"Where has this magnificent workbook been hiding? Bill Knaus, or. friendly guide. This time it is about managing anger. It is a crucially important read during this unprecedented period, which has given birth to heightened levels of fear, frustration, and anger. Bravo, Bill Knaus!"

> —**Barry Lubetkin, PhD**, past president of The American Board of Behavioral Psychology, and coauthor of *Why Do I Need You to Love Me in Order to Like Myself?*

"This user-friendly, five-star book beautifully covers the cognitive and behavioral steps proven to be effective in anger management. Bill Knaus correctly emphasizes one of Albert Ellis' most significant contributions: the evocative role of low frustration tolerance in emotional distress, and how to reduce anger and distress by increasing frustration tolerance. He describes how you can arrive at a deeply internalized understanding of the seemingly 'simple' but rarely arrived at belief that 'you can't get through to everyone.'"

> —**Janet L. Wolfe, PhD**, author of *What to Do When He Has a Headache*, and executive director of the Albert Ellis Institute for more than thirty years

"After I read Bill Knaus's *The Cognitive Behavioral Workbook for Anger*, I realized that this is not merely a self-help text to deal with anger. Knaus successfully combines the top scholarship dedicated to this topic with an applied bent accessible to anyone who has anger issues or who consults with clients with anger problems. Undoubtedly, Knaus's workbook represents a tour de force of penetrating insights, unquestionable scholarship, and practical reasoning."

> —**S. Zinaich, Jr., PhD**, professor at Purdue University Northwest, author of numerous articles on philosophical counseling, and associate executive director of the National Philosophical Counseling Association

"When I read *The Cognitive Behavioral Workbook for Anger*, I felt as if Bill Knaus was sitting in a comfortable chair in my living room speaking to me. In language that is easily understood, he explains the thoughts of other great thinkers, from Epictetus to Ellis, and offers remarkably practical ideas about the roots of anger and what works to change old patterns. I love useful books. This is one."

> —**Derek Paar, PhD**, licensed psychologist, and emeritus professor at Springfield College

"Despite its enduring role in conflicts and emotional distress, anger continues to be poorly addressed. Most who attempt to help others with anger control problems do so without evidenced-based methods. Bill Knaus's *The Cognitive Behavioral Workbook for Anger* resolves these deficiencies. Practically anyone can use this guide to understand the origins of anger, discover the triggers that can elicit it, and see how to apply practical tools to cope effectively with anger and anger-related problems. I strongly recommend this book for helping professionals and people wanting sensible self-help solutions to anger problems."

> —**Michael Abrams, PhD, ABPP**, adjunct full professor at New York University, and author of *The New CBT*

"Bill Knaus has distilled his decades of clinical experience, teaching, and authoring twenty-five self-help books into this cogent and compelling volume: *The Cognitive Behavioral Workbook for Anger*! Having facilitated almost 800 SMART Recovery and Inside Out meetings in prisons and jails worldwide, I have concluded that unconstrained anger causes almost as many incarcerations as addictions. This workbook is an accessible and engaging approach to enhancing control of destructive anger."

> —**Joseph Gerstein, MD, FACP**, clinical assistant professor of medicine at Harvard Medical School, and founding president of the SMART Recovery Mutual-Aid Group Program

"Anger is the individual, social, relational, political, and psychological cancer of the contemporary age. Bill Knaus's workbook is the penultimate cognitive behavioral scalpel to excise this *tumor*. What is remarkable about his approach is that he individualizes both the situations, categories, and interventions that may be used by clinicians, patients, or readers to be anger management masters. Outstanding!"

> —**George Morelli, PhD**, Center for Cognitive Therapy of North County San Diego

"Bill Knaus is at the forefront of CBT, developing techniques and working alongside its founders, including Albert Ellis, for decades. This workbook is a clear guide to overcoming destructive anger, that tricky and confusing emotion. Bill Knaus has developed a practical, evidence-based program. His new workbook is a wise and encouraging guide to mastering the destructive parts of anger."

> —**Nando Pelusi, PhD**, cofounder of the Applied Evolutionary Psychology Society (AEPS), and contributing editor at *Psychology Today*

"Open the book. Bill Knaus brings an insightful, commonsense, wise approach to overcome destructive forms of anger and aggression, and to use anger productively in exasperating times. Try Knaus's practical hints and experiments to navigate past excessive anger and the complex emotions and cognitions of frustration and stress that often fuse with this emotion. Use the worksheets to stay on track. You can still thrive in exasperating times by putting destructive anger into the rearview mirror of your life."

—**Michael F. Shaughnessy, PhD**, professor of psychology at Eastern New Mexico University

"Bill Knaus has taken his self-mastery approach to another key issue—anger. The book provides a simple breakdown of the issues that produce what he calls 'parasitic anger.' It provides a series of exercises designed to help a person work through harmful forms of anger with tested methods to guide the reader's efforts. Although beneficial for self-helpers, this book can be a valuable resource for those combating anger problems in CBT therapy."

—**James W. Thompson, PhD, MBA**, retired naval reserve officer who served in the Air Force
and Army as an organizational effectiveness officer, clinical psychologist, psychometrist,
and rational emotive behavioral therapy (REBT) therapist

"Bill Knaus has brilliantly tackled what is arguably the world's biggest problem. Anger is the root cause of enormous human suffering and the primary source of hostility, hatred, bigotry, divorce, assault, murder, and mass destruction. Bill shows how to reduce anger down to a very manageable level. If you choose to eliminate destructive anger from your life, this is the guide to do it. Imagine replacing hostile aggression with elevating the positive potential of our species. What a different world that would be."

—**Vincent E. Parr, PhD**, psychologist in private practice in Tampa, FL;
and author of *You Only Have Four Problems*

"This is the workbook you've been looking for! All humans have gotten angry at times, but how many have prepared themselves to appropriately manage anger? Bill Knaus has given us all a comprehensive gift—a collection of cognitive behavioral tools to help live more fully and wisely by reducing, or eliminating, the sort of anger that destroys relationships and inner peace. Read the book and see."

—**Deborah Steinberg, MSW**, supervisor at the Albert Ellis Institute,
coauthor of *How to Stick to a Diet*, and group facilitator of Judaism and Mindfulness
at New Synagogue of Palm Beach in Florida

"Was I the only one who believed in fairness? Did unfairness force me to feel angry? I read two draft chapters on fairness and perspective from this book. I had an epiphany. Unfair things happen. I can't control that. I can do my best to fix things without expecting perfection. That perspective lowered my anger temperature considerably. I can't wait to read the rest of the book."

—**LBD**, student of self-help

"Bill Knaus's book overflows with gems, and one of them is learning to assertively motivate others to accede to your requests without infringing on their rights. But first you'll learn to lower your anger temperature. Pulling together a broad anger literature, his extensive experience helping others with anger problems, and core principles from Albert Ellis's pioneering REBT, Bill boils down anger causes, forms, and shades, and shows how to free yourself from a lifetime of suffering from irrational anger. Read the book and see."

—**Michael R. Edelstein, PhD**, clinical psychologist, author of *Three Minute Therapy*, and one of the primary postdoctoral fellows in REBT

"Do you want to stop feeling angry? If you do, you'll find a friendly guide in Bill Knaus as you go on this challenging adventure. You'll learn wise ways to cut loose from anger, build skills to express yourself well, and live your life free from needless conflicts and stress. What's next? Pass on what you know to help others ease their anger burdens. Everyone wins when working together."

—**Jack Shannon, EdD**, psychologist in private practice in Matawan, NJ; and professor emeritus at Seton Hall University

"Anger can have a devastating impact upon relationships, and also a detrimental effect upon both mental and physical health. In twelve chapters, *The Cognitive Behavioral Workbook for Anger* provides an exciting, step-by-step self-coaching program to tackle anger head-on. It delivers a straightforward, ABCD framework to modify your anger and destructive behaviors. This workbook includes many useful anger-busting techniques and exercises. These methods could change your life!"

—**Stephen Palmer, PhD**, professor of practice at the University of Wales Trinity Saint David in Wales, UK; and founder director of the Centre for Stress Management in London, England, UK

The
Cognitive
Behavioral
Workbook
for
Anger

A STEP-BY-STEP PROGRAM *for* SUCCESS

WILLIAM J. KNAUS, EdD

Impact Publishers, Inc.

Publisher's Note

NEW HARBINGER PUBLICATIONS is a registered trademark of New Harbinger Publications, Inc.

New Harbinger Publications is an employee-owned company

Distributed in Canada by Raincoast Books

Copyright © 2021 by William J. Knaus
      New Harbinger Publications, Inc.
      5674 Shattuck Avenue
      Oakland, CA 94609
      www.newharbinger.com

Cover design by Amy Shoup

Acquired by Jess O'Brien

Edited by Rona Bernstein

All Rights Reserved

Library of Congress Cataloging-in-Publication Data on file

Printed in the United States of America

25   24   23

10   9   8   7   6   5   4

I dedicate this book to my fallen friends, Janet Cohan, Rina Cohan, Bud Gaiennie, Al Granfield, Jon Edgerly, Frank Eldridge, George Elias, Forrest Patenaude, Leon Pomeroy, Dick Sprinthall, and my friend and cousin, Tom Murphy. Our ranks are thinning, my old friends. I miss you all.

Contents

Acknowledgments   vii

Foreword   ix

Introduction   1

1   Anger Angles   7

2   Six Ways to Combat Anger   29

3   Pathways to Positive Change   43

4   Your Perspective Solution   55

5   Coping with Unfairness   69

6   Body-Mind Solutions   87

7   The Frustration-Tension Tolerance Solution   107

8   Problem-Solving Solutions   119

9   Assertive Solutions   129

10   How to Communicate Effectively with Impact   139

11   Mastery over Anger   151

12   Top Tips from Anger Experts   163

References   177

Index   191

Acknowledgments

My special thanks and gratitude go to Dr. Irwin Altrows for his many valued contributions to this project. My special thanks and gratitude go to my wife, Dr. Nancy Knaus, who flagged typos and commented on the content. Both Irwin and Nancy were invaluable to me on this project, and the book is better for their efforts.

I especially appreciate the efforts of each person who contributed a tip to help people struggling with anger. Each gave their top tips to point the way to a better future free of the burdens of needless anger. My special thanks and gratitude (in random order) go to Ed Garcia, Dr. Norman Cotterell, Jimmy Walter, Dr. Diana Richman, Dr. Pam Garcy, Anonymous, Dr. Sam Klarreich, Dr. Bill Golden, Dr. Stefan Hofmann, Dr. Elliot Cohen, Dr. Jeff Rudolph, Dr. Joel Block, Dr. William Knaus II, MD, Dr. Roberta Galluccio Richardson, Dr. Russ Grieger, Dr. Shawn Blau, and Dr. Howie Kassinove.

Foreword

Every book about anger—Amazon tells us there are thousands of them—has a slightly different take on the topic. *Express it, or don't. Understand it, or forget about it. Meditate over it, or hit pillows. Accept it, or explain it away. Kick the habit, or kick the dog. Throw something, or take a deep breath. Shout out your feelings, or stay quiet.*

So why should you read this book over all the others? What does Bill Knaus have to offer that others don't? Is there anything new here? *The Cognitive Behavioral Workbook for Anger* is different. Let me tell you why it's better.

First of all, Bill Knaus is the real deal. He's a highly qualified psychologist with decades of experience in helping folks deal with the issues that disrupt, discomfit, disturb, and discombobulate their lives. I've known Bill for many years, and I know he knows what works to make things better.

Second, Bill's approach is practical, down-to-earth, empirically proven, and within reach. It doesn't require months of exercises or years of therapy. (It's not a silver bullet, however, and it will require you to do some work.)

Third, Bill doesn't ask you to believe in a magical cure. He acknowledges that anger is a tough nut to crack. He knows you can't just close your eyes and make it go away. He encourages you (and gives you the tools) to figure out what's happening around the anger in *your* life. And he offers a wide variety of proven solutions you can apply to develop your own skills—what works for you—in dealing with your problem anger.

Fourth, if you work it right, you'll gain from this book a thorough grounding in the basics of cognitive behavioral therapy; awareness of nine key factors of anger; guidance in self-examination and reappraisal of your ideas about anger; expansion and application of what you learn, through worksheets and skill-building exercises; and a structure to help you stay on course as you learn, a "progress log."

And there's more. This volume covers what's known about anger (and what you think you know that's not so), and the important differences between *natural* (positive, constructive) and *parasitic* (toxic, problem) anger. Especially important and valuable in the cognitive behavioral formulation is the notion of cognitive restructuring: the process of reframing your response to anger-provoking situations so as to respond to them most constructively.

Cognitive behavioral therapy is derived from the rational emotive behavior therapy system, which was created by famed psychologist Dr. Albert Ellis. Dr. Ellis was fond of quoting the first-century Greek philosopher Epictetus: "What disturbs people's minds is not events, but their judgments on events." You'll discover in the chapters that follow just how much difference your judgments on events make in your daily interactions with others. In short, *you get angry because of the way you look at things.*

I've been a researcher, teacher, therapist, and author focusing on constructive self-expression (including anger) for more than forty years, from the days of pillow-pounding and Bobo dolls; through self-awareness exercises; to behavioral skills training; and to meditation, mindfulness, acceptance and commitment, and beyond. It's clear to me that anger will always be an element of the human experience.

I've found that what we know about anger can be described in a handful of key tenets:

- Anger is a natural, normal, human emotion, not a style of behavior.

- A modest level of anger arousal is healthy—a signal that there is a problem to solve.

- Chronic anger can be a major health hazard.

- We can—and should—learn to defuse most anger, even before it begins.

- We get angry because of the way we look at things—our thoughts, values, and beliefs.

- When we must express anger, it's best to work toward resolution, not revenge.

- No system or approach to dealing with anger works for everybody all the time.

One of the great things about a workbook is that it can be a sort of structured diary or journal, giving you space to keep track of your progress and forcing you to think about questions you might otherwise avoid. Like a diary, nobody else sees it unless you want them to. You're completely free to record your answers, thoughts, fears, and issues.

Think through the concepts you learn here. Complete the exercises. Answer the questions. Fill in the blanks. Write in the margins. Above all, be honest with yourself. *The Cognitive Behavioral Workbook for Anger* is your definitive guide, a powerful tool that can motivate, structure, and record your journey from parasitic to natural anger expression. Put it to work for you.

—Robert Alberti, coauthor of *Your Perfect Right*

Introduction

If you are among the millions of people whose anger creates unwanted troubles, read on. If you have too many reasons to feel angry, you'll see how to whittle them down. Maybe you are tired of feeling angry and want to live a calmer life. This book covers that, too. And it will also show you how to protect yourself from others' anger.

When is anger a problem for you? Anger is a problem when you think it is. But that's not the full story. Two or more significant destructive aggressive actions, in different places and times, suggest a pattern. So when is your anger worth addressing?

- When you feel angered too often, in too many ways, and to a harmful extreme

- When it negatively affects the quality of your life

- When your anger is affecting those close to you

It can take just one explosive anger incident to capsize your life. That risk is worth preventing.

In this book, I refer to forms of anger that drain time, resources, and energy as *parasitic anger*. If you think anger is a problem for you and is harmful in the way that a parasite is, are you ready to take steps to lessen it? If your answer is yes, be assured that you have many ways to do this.

This book will teach you how to prevent or lessen parasitic forms of anger by using proven techniques based on a form of therapy called cognitive behavioral therapy (CBT). After we look at a brief history of CBT and see why it is effective, I'll describe how to become a self-help expert in using CBT to build positive skills by combatting destructive forms of anger. Throughout the book, you'll find numerous techniques and exercises to help you on this path. Several of these are available to download on the website for this book, http://www.newharbinger.com/44321. (See the very back of this book for more details.) By selecting CBT methods that apply to your situation and practicing them, you can learn to free yourself from false beliefs, develop new healthy beliefs, experience more positive emotions, and live your life less angrily and far more productively.

A BRIEF CBT HISTORY

The phrase "cognitive behavioral therapy" appeared around 1970 as an umbrella term for a system developed to overcome negative conditions such as anger, anxiety, and depression. Since that time, millions have used CBT methods to address practically every psychological affliction. Although it is a relatively new term, various CBT methods have been around for over 2,400 years. CBT owes a debt of gratitude to the Greek philosopher Socrates and to the ancient Stoics, whom I consider to be early cognitive therapists.

Around 400 BCE, Socrates developed a purposeful, open-ended questioning method for helping people understand and educate themselves. Today, Socratic questioning is a research-supported CBT method for deconstructing harmful false beliefs (Clark and Eagen 2015; Heiniger, Clark, and Egan 2017). Here is an example of how you can use questions to gain clarity: You angrily believe that people are out to get you. You ask yourself, *Among the seven billion people who live on this planet, where is the evidence that they all think the same way about me?* The answer? There is no evidence for that.

The ancient Stoics explored the influence of thinking on emotions and mental health. Starting with the founder of the Stoic movement, Zeno (circa 300 BCE), the Stoics devised reasoning methods to correct distressful false thinking that cognitive behavioral therapists use today (Robertson 2010). Ancients who lived the Stoic way appear to have found greater inner peace compared to those who magnified and muddled their thinking about the significance of events. Thus, the Stoics were free to experience a broader range of emotions.

Stoics viewed emotions as "things which follow upon judgments" (Graver 2007, 29). They found that events need not dictate a specific form of thought. They explored how false beliefs and misjudgments promote emotional excesses. They studied and taught others how to see and rid themselves of false beliefs. They devised ways to accept adversity, hardship, and matters outside of their control. They displayed curiosity about natural emotions, such as anger, and about acting on natural emotions that were free from false beliefs and misjudgments. They pursued living responsible, simple, humble lives (consolidated from Graver 2007). The Stoics' views influenced the work of many scholars, psychiatrists, and psychologists whose efforts were on improving psychological health.

You'll also find Buddhist teachings in CBT. Here are a few: You deepen your understanding of yourself by knowledge of how your mind works. You accept things as they are. You replace unpleasant thoughts with positive ones. You act honorably, as this is in the enlightened interest of all. With meditation, you cultivate wisdom and compassion from insights. The enemies of enlightenment are lies, dishonest dealings, abusive language, and harming others. Nothing lasts. All things change.

The Theravada Buddhism scriptures (written between 300 BCE and 100 BCE) cite Gautama Buddha's teachings on reducing anger to help the self and society with three steps: (1) nonresponse to provocations, (2) kindness, and (3) the right intention to avoid violence and revenge. These three points have modern scientific support (Ariyabuddhiphongs 2014).

You can also find CBT principles and practices in the work of many early- to mid-twentieth-century therapists and theorists who independently connected the dots between thinking and feeling and doing. Their work led to the understanding that negative thinking triggered negative emotions and harmful behavior—and that we can change negative thinking through reeducation (Dubois 1909b; Williams 1914, 1923). They developed behavioral conditioning methods to help children overcome fears and phobias (Jones 1924) and to help people free themselves from needless inhibitions (Salter 1949).

Pioneers in the field recognized the destructive force of negative anger-arousing evaluations and offered practical solutions (Ellis 1977; Beck 1999). Many twentieth-century pioneers saw that not only could you change how you feel by changing your thinking, but also you could change your thinking and feelings by changing what you do.

CBT is like a living sponge, growing by absorbing new evidence-based techniques and systems all the time. Arnold Lazarus's multi-modal therapy (MMT), psychologist Steven Hayes's acceptance and commitment therapy (ACT), and Zindel Segal and John Teasdale's mindfulness-based cognitive behavior therapy (MBCBT) operate separately from CBT but also broaden the base of the CBT system.

RESEARCH SUPPORT FOR CBT

CBT has more favorable outcome studies and more meta-analyses (studies of studies used to find patterns and trends in the data) than any other psychological therapy approach, making it the gold standard therapy system. I informally reviewed 501 CBT meta-analyses, which collectively demonstrate that the CBT approach has the strongest support for reducing anger, anxiety, depression, posttraumatic stress disorder, and other difficulties, such as sleep disorders and perfectionism. Boston University psychology professor Stefan Hofmann (Hofmann and Asmundson 2017) scientifically studied 106 CBT meta-analyses and found persuasive support for CBT interventions for reducing anxiety, anger, and general stress.

GROWTH BY READING

Can you use CBT readings to improve your life? Studies show that indeed you can. Bibliotherapy is the use of books (e.g., self-help books) as therapy to treat psychological conditions. I reviewed 158 scholarly articles on CBT bibliotherapy, the majority of which showed positive results for people working on their own or with professional guidance. Improvements from this "healing through reading" approach seem lasting, and changes in one area can favorably affect a problem-related area (Wootton et al. 2018; Spinhoven et al. 2018).

How do you select self-help books? Chapman University professor Richard Redding recommended single-topic books authored by professionally trained doctoral level mental health experts. Redding found that the highest-rated self-help books highlighted cognitive behavioral methods (Redding et al. 2008). The book you have in your hands—*The Cognitive Behavioral Workbook for Anger*—meets these standards.

Here are six potential benefits of using this CBT workbook to combat parasitic forms of anger:

1. You can learn pretested self-help ideas in a reasonably short time.

2. You have access to many professionally designed self-improvement experiments.

3. You are free to choose what you'll do based on what is relevant to you.

4. You can work at your own pace.

5. You can highlight important parts in the book and go over them as many times as you wish.

6. You can modify experiments to suit your situation and use the results to make adjustments.

GROWTH BY DOING

Two important components of CBT are (1) gaining information that helps promote new understandings and perspectives and (2) completing behavioral assignments. First, in order to learn strategies to reduce anger, it is important to know:

- how thinking and believing affect feelings;

- how problem anger co-occurs with other problems, such as anxiety, negative mood, hunger, and fear;

- how to target and reduce anger; and

- how to recognize parasitic anger thinking and mute its effects when you experience these thoughts.

Second, behavioral practice sessions (behavioral assignments) are at the heart of any active self-improvement approach and are one of the most important parts of CBT (Kazantzis et al. 2018). Albert Ellis (1962), a grandfather of CBT, strongly emphasized doing "homework assignments" to test ideas in practical settings. Here you experiment with new ways of thinking, feeling, and doing; measure the results of what you do; and make adjustments based on the feedback you get. How else are you to improve?

You'll find this interactive workbook loaded with cognitive (thinking), emotive (feeling), and behavioral (doing) experiments. Pick the ones that seem right for you. These are your self-selected behavioral assignments.

How much time does it take to learn and practice CBT methods to make a positive personal change with anger? There are no hard and fast rules. Different people are at different stages of change. Problems vary as do life circumstances. There are so many varieties, nuances, and conditions for anger that it is impractical to consider them all in this book. You'll sometimes have to adapt methods to special anger problem areas. For example, if I had more space to write, I'd have loved to write a chapter on "Anger and Quarreling Couples." However, if you spend half as much time per week as you would on a three-credit college history course, you are likely to make noteworthy positive progress in four months. Experiment. Adjust the time up or down.

PATHS TO SELF-MASTERY

Self-mastery boils down to having a realistic sense of command over yourself and the controllable events around you. By meeting both everyday and significant life challenges, you can learn much about your capabilities for dealing with adversities and pursuing positive opportunities. Personal change is a self-mastery process—not an event. Surprisingly, learning to address needless forms of anger is as good a way as any to move toward self-mastery. Self-mastery builds on three pillars for self-learning: no failure, no blame, and preparation. These pillars support the stage for developing and using cognitive, emotive, and behavioral change approaches to combat parasitic anger.

The No-Failure Way

Effective therapists help promote realistic awareness in their clients and serve as catalysts for productive actions. You can follow this same awareness-action direction for overcoming parasitic forms of anger. However, this takes developing knowledge and experimenting with solutions. Let's turn to that next.

Failure is part of life. You may fail to get a job you want, date the person of your dreams, or pass an entry test. The consequences for such failures are hardly fatal; the odds are you will bounce back and try again or try a different way. It's a learning process. A no-failure approach involves seeing failures as opportunities for learning. When you apply a no-failure approach to your self-mastery efforts, you are doing so to discover what works, what doesn't, and how you might improve. You put on your scientist's hat and experiment. You don't judge yourself globally. Rather, you judge the processes and results. You figure out what works best for you to reduce or rid yourself of parasitic forms of anger.

Thomas Edison expressed this view when it came to his inventions. Once asked how he could tolerate so many failures to find a filament for a light bulb, Edison answered unexpectedly. He said he discovered what didn't work.

The No-Blame Way

If you sideswipe a fender of a legally parked car, you are to blame and bear responsibility for the cost of the repair. If blame stayed at this level, humanity would be far less affected by the consequences of anger. However, very often people blow legitimate gripes out of proportion by blaming and condemning. Throughout this book, you'll see how to advance your positive interests and rights productively without excessive blame.

The Preparation Way

A top artist, mechanic, teacher, or manager hones many skills over a lifetime. Developing these skills takes countless hours of practice, much of which involves mental practice fused with physically polishing behavioral skills. Likewise, mental preparation to cope with anger takes time, practice, and honing skills in the form of blending objective ways of thinking with problem-solving actions. I coined the phrase "mental karate" to describe this process. The key is to experiment with approaches that fit your personality and situation. As the old adage goes, "An ounce of prevention is worth a pound of cure."

Over the past several thousand years, many wise people saw the personal, social, and health dangers of excessive and extreme anger and aggression. We are fortunate to have many fine-minded contemporary thinkers with solutions for overcoming problematic anger. Some contributed their top tips for this book, which you'll find throughout the chapters, including chapter 12, where you'll find a collection of tips covering diverse anger topics.

WHAT WORKS FOR YOU?

One size does not fit all, and what works for you in one situation may not in another. Not everyone wears the same-sized shirt or prefers the same colors and design. Nevertheless, shirts have features in common, as do CBT anger-reduction approaches. Some will apply better in some situations, like a long-sleeved T-shirt for a hike on a chilly day and a button-down shirt for a formal party.

Throughout this book you'll find dozens of ways to overcome parasitic anger. Some might make a significant impact. Others may make a small difference. However, a small change is not a negligible change. Many small changes add up. Along with the larger changes, they are part of an accumulation effect for progress. Also keep in mind that people change at different rates. A lot depends on readiness and strength of motivation. Lapses and spurts and treading water occur along the way. Some go at a gradual pace. Others move in spurts in the beginning and pace themselves differently later.

Once you set your mind on accomplishing something of importance—in this case, reducing the harmful effects of anger—you'll find ideas that support that interest everywhere (Payot 1909). Eventually, you'll develop a coping frame of reference or a tested array of ways to prevent and combat anger problems tailor-made for you. As you master the methods that seem right for you, you might experience sudden gains (Tang et al. 2005). When these leaps occur, they often correspond with a reduction in negative thinking (Wiedemann et al. 2020). I stacked the book with ideas to reduce negative thinking.

You are the captain of your ship, steering your course through the waters of life. You can do a lot on your own to move in healthier, happier, positive directions. However, if you have a serious anger crisis, you don't have to do it all by yourself. A CBT counselor, like a harbormaster, can help point to treacherous waters and show you how to get past the obstacles. If you are already working with a professional counselor on anger, you can use *The Cognitive Behavioral Workbook for Anger* to support and speed your progress.

CHAPTER 1

Anger Angles

Anger often gets an undeserved bad rap as a destructive prelude to aggression. Frederick Tracy, an early pioneer in psychology, had a different view. He saw anger as "a force which education should direct and not annihilate" (1896, 47). The problem with anger lies in its abuse.

Let's look at two examples of anger. In the first one, you see a parent beating a child for crying and feel a protective sense of anger. In the second example, you misplace your keys, look for someone else to blame, and throw a tantrum. Think of these examples as two sides of a coin. On one side of the coin, you'll find *natural anger*. It's a mobilizing force against a threat. It's a pushback emotion against unfairness and inequities. It's an expression of dominance. You show natural anger to control another's adverse behaviors. You don't need words to express natural anger. Natural anger has been around for over 200,000 years, before the days of language as we know it today. On the opposite side of the coin is *parasitic anger*. This form of anger acts like a parasite, draining your mental and emotional resources. This anger is an automatic response to some triggering event that has little to do with surviving, thriving, building friendships, or much of anything else that is positive.

How do you liberate yourself from parasitic anger? You'll start your journey in this chapter, where we'll cover

- a survey for skills you want to improve or develop that apply to lessening needless anger,

- nine anger factors,

- four main purposes that anger serves, and

- solutions to handling anger emergencies and tested ways to quell harmful forms of anger before things get out of hand, including three primary levels for change.

An early twentieth-century psychologist saw anger this way:

The problem with anger lies not in its existence but rather in the difficulties in controlling and directing it and limiting it to its proper function; while not properly disciplined, it, of course, introduces disorder and pain into the mental life. (Cooley 1902, 252–253)

Anger is the most complex and controversial of the different primal emotions. It is often the most dreaded emotion—mainly because of the aggressiveness, intimidation, violence, hostility, ill will, and unpleasantries commonly associated with it.

How pervasive is anger? In a 2017 American Psychological Association stress survey, 35% of those responding reported irritability and anger as a result of stress as a problem, with 7.8% reporting outbursts and aggressive actions of yelling, hitting, or throwing objects (Okuda et al. 2015).

If anger is a problem for you, where do you start to get a handle on what you can do? The following anger survey can help identify skill areas that apply to overcoming parasitic anger. (You can also download this survey from the website for this book, http://www.newharbinger.com/44321.)

ANGER SURVEY

Although this survey doesn't cover every conceivable anger angle, it applies to what you'll find in this book and will help you identify important areas for you to concentrate on.

Instructions: When you come to a statement that sounds like a skill you'd like to advance, put a checkmark in the "Yes" column. In column three, you'll find the chapters in the book that refer to related skills.

Item	Yes	Chapters for Corrective Actions
1. If I could take time to cool down, I would.	✓	1
2. I'd like to be able to stop my anger from getting out of control.	✓	1
3. I'd like to know the deeper causes for my anger.	✓	1
4. I'd like to know if yelling and screaming will help release anger and tension.	✓	2
5. If I had a way to stop blaming others, I'd do it.		2
6. I'd like to feel more tolerant.		2
7. I'd like to know more about changing my angry thinking.	✓	3
8. I want to stop repeating the same anger problems.	✓	3
9. If there were a solution as simple as ABC, I'd use it.	✓	3
10. When I lose perspective, I'd like to get it back.	✓	4

11. I want to use my reasoning skills more effectively.	✔	4
12. Rather than having my thoughts blurred by anger, I'd like to think with clarity.	✔	4
13. When someone treats me unfairly, I'd like to respond effectively.	✔	5
14. I'm too distrusting at times, and I'd like to change that.		5
15. I want to be fair in my use of words.		5
16. I'm too often stressed, and I'd like to feel calmer.	✔	6
17. I have poor sleep patterns, and I'd like to fix that.		6
18. I'm concerned that too much anger will hurt my health, and I'd like to reduce that risk.	✔	6
19. I'm too easily frustrated and would like to get over that.	✔	7
20. I can unsettle myself by making too much of a minor situation, and want to keep things in perspective.	✔	7
21. I know I need to be more reflective and would like to learn some new techniques.		7
22. I have many anger problems and not enough solutions, and I'm open to new problem-solving ideas.	✔	8
23. If I could treat anger as a solvable problem, I would.		8
24. I wish I could pull the plug on anger before I start raging.		8
25. There are times I need to advocate for myself nonangrily.	✔	9
26. I want to assert my interests forcefully but not aggressively.		9
27. I know I need to think beyond the moment in tough situations.		9
28. I tend to jump to conclusions, and I'd like to do that less often.		10
29. I know I need to be a better listener.		10
30. It'd solve a lot of my problems if I communicated clearly.		10
31. I'm too reactive at times and would prefer to slow down.		11
32. I know what to do but keep falling back to old anger habits.		11
33. If I had a map for changing, I'd follow it.		11
34. I want to be able to estimate what anger costs and how to lessen the price.		12
35. I know I need to do more work looking at different angles before acting.		12
36. I'd like to act quicker in considering my choices in anger situations.		12

Before we dive into how to reduce anger, it's important to identify your reasons for doing so. Take a few minutes to give this some thought.

What are your incentives for attacking a parasitic anger problem? For example, what painful consequences would you avoid? (Avoiding pain is positive.) What would you gain? (Achieving a healthy result is positive.) In the box below, pencil in one to three main incentives for breaking a parasitic anger pattern.

1.

2.

3.

Seeing things in writing, such as in the box above, can sometimes strengthen your incentive to act.

NINE ANGER FACTORS

Let's look more closely at the natural and parasitic sides of the anger coin.

Natural anger is an externalizing emotion. With natural anger, you feel aroused to meet a threat. Your sympathetic nervous system charges your body with hormones to go on the offense. Your focus narrows on the external triggers of anger because this is efficient when you face danger.

Most harmful anger is of the parasitic anger variety. Parasitic anger-evoking beliefs, such as "I must be in control," "I must be smarter than everybody," and "The world should comply with my wishes" give meaning to the situations that evoke them, giving them the power to trigger and amplify anger feelings and aggressive action when someone threatens these ego beliefs.

Parasitic blame is a common driving force in anger. Anger is normally an externalized emotion of going against something or somebody. Most accept reality for what they believe they see without realizing that we all orchestrate our experiences from within. For example, blame is normally an externalizing belief that can evoke anger when blame extends into condemnation. You blame another driver for driving too slowly; that justifies running the driver off the road.

Anger can turn inward. You suppress anger by trying to bury the emotion for fear of social consequences, fear of retaliation if you express anger, fear of losing control, believing it is impolite to express anger, and more. You also turn anger against yourself when you are hypercritical and blame yourself for every imperfection.

Anger is an unrecognized shadow emotion. Anger co-occurs with and adds to the severity of down moods, anxiety, and other unpleasant states (Cassiello-Robbins and Barlow 2016). Anger can precede, prolong, and amplify the misery of depression. The good news is that by lessening anger, you may reduce depression and anxiety when these three conditions merge (Kim 2018).

Anger affects memory and can promote tunnel vision. Anger tends to impede your memory, causing you to remember fewer details. This loss can place limits on the information you have in your memory for self-correction. High-intensity anger narrows your ability to assess complex situations. Thus, higher levels of anger are perfect storm conditions for repeating a parasitic anger pattern and gathering more poor results.

Anger and hostility are different but related. You can be angry without being hostile. For example, if physically attacked, you angrily strike back. This protective action is normal, functional, and temporary. Hostility is a lingering, bitter, vengeful feeling fused with thoughts to cause harm. Hostility includes antagonistic acts and pleasure at others' misery. A natural anger toward another's hostility is normally appropriate.

Anger and aggression are related but different. Anger is an emotion. Aggression is a behavioral expression of anger or hostility that comes in different forms: a natural, protective action against a threat; an act to intentionally cause harm to others; or an intimidating act to gain benefits.

Aggression and assertiveness are both ways to respond to a problem. Aggression, especially aggression blinded by hostility and advanced by rage, is a red flag. Aggression is an impulse to hurt, often with little, if any, reflection. On the other hand, assertiveness is more of a reflective judgment about a situation and about doing just enough to bring about the change you want, without needlessly harming others.

It's important to understand these nine factors and how they apply to your own anger as you proceed on this journey to reduce your anger. It's also important to look at anger from different views.

FOUR VIEWS OF ANGER

When you think of anger, you might think of how people look, how they posture themselves, and the timber and tone of speech connected to the emotion. But are you thinking stereotypically? You can also find variability between people in their social expressions of anger. In fact, some people smile when they're angry. And the same person may show variations in anger expression over the course of the same situation. Context, of course, is important.

Anger is complex. Anger can be a signal, a symptom, a protection, and a problem habit. Let's explore these four views.

Anger is a signal. Anger signals others to back off. Anger's facial expression, posturing, and vocal tones emphasize this intent. About 200,000 years ago, anger signals served another purpose. If your group was threatened by a predator or another group and you perceived that fight was better than flight, you'd emit an anger signal, which would alert the others to gather and defend.

Anger is a symptom. Anger co-occurs with depression about 50% of the time and is common among those with social anxiety, general anxiety, and shame. Anger can also be a symptom of hunger, lack of sleep, the onset of the flu, and so forth. The challenge is to read the signal right and address the right problem.

Anger is a protection. An aroused anger is a biologically charged state to advance against a threat. Anger can also drive someone to correct an inequity or protect a vulnerable person from harm.

Anger is a problem habit. Some forms of anger (i.e., parasitic angers) reflect negative patterns of thought aroused in situations you view as unacceptable hassles, challenges to your ego, violations of your expectations, and so on. These conditions of the mind are close to the surface of your awareness yet elude detection and therefore will go on until you make them conscious and alter their automatic course.

Researchers who study anger use labels such as *anger-in* and *anger-out* to refer to the direction of anger; *trait* and *state* refer to an inborn tendency for excess anger versus anger that is more situational. These anger labels are useful if you plan to research an anger area.

Here is the big issue: If you are inclined to lessen the stresses and strains and fallout from excess anger, what do you do? Let's start figuring that out.

If you have social anxiety, and you dread others judging you, you might anger yourself because you think others think wrongly of you. Anger defenses show up in other ways, too. To feel comfortable and in control, you demand conformity from others. Therein lies the terror and the error in a fictional fear of loss of control.

Top Tip: Clear the View

When anger is your way of coping with fear and controlling others, who's in charge of changing that? Ed Garcia, a ninety-one-year-old Atlanta, Georgia, artist and psychotherapist, tackles this anger-fear puzzle.

Does an ongoing anger pattern show toughness? Not really. In some situations, you protect yourself by trying to control others to gain power over your fears. Where's the strength in holding on to a problem? Without changing yourself, you have little hope for freedom from this pattern.

By doing what you fear, you show toughness. For example, if you usually feel anger when someone disagrees with you, what do you have to fear? Do something different. Find a point of agreement and say, "I agree with that." Take a simple step like that, and you've opened yourself to a flexible view. By acknowledging a problem, accepting your responsibility, and then doing something, you put yourself on a path to positive change. Now, that's real toughness.

EMERGENCY RESPONSES

In the beginning stages of change, you are likely to have your share of anger emergencies. Let's look at some start-up coping methods to contain the different forms of parasitic anger. We'll start with the walking solution.

The Walking Solution

To discover how the walking solution works, we'll learn about Dan and how he used the approach.

On his way home from his job, Dan felt his anger temperature rising. He felt flushed and had tensed muscles and a quickened heartbeat. What was going on? His day did not go perfectly. He had many problems to solve, and others took for granted he'd solve them. It was that way every day.

Dan thought he didn't get the respect and appreciation he deserved (and should have) from ungrateful customers and a boss who took his skills for granted. As he neared his home, Dan's thoughts switched to his wife and kids. He thought, They take me for granted. I'm a meal ticket. *He regularly defaulted to this line of thinking.*

As had been going on for years, Dan entered his home in a frightening angry mood. He saw toys on the floor. He yelled at his kids: "Pick up that crap, or it goes to the trash." He turned to his wife and yelled, "Why isn't my dinner on the table!" If he didn't find toys on the floor, it was something else. The TV was too loud. The kids were not studying enough. His wife should learn a thing or two about dressing right. About a half-hour after the daily anger tirade, Dan calmed down, felt guilty, and swore to himself, I won't do that again. *That was a well-meaning but false promise.*

Dan's wife came to a breaking point. One day, with an unusually strong determination in her voice, she told him, "Whatever your problems are, they are not with us. You need to deal with them, or there will be no more us."

He and his wife had talked about his anger before. This time Dan knew she meant business. Dan's incentive for change was to spare his family from abuse at his hands and preserve his relationship with the people he loved the most. It was a strong incentive.

The walking solution is a simple start-up method to buy time and think things through. You take a fifteen-minute walk and separate the different physical parts of your anger sensations. Then you log what you are thinking and identify the thoughts that fuse with the angry feelings.

The next time Dan had a tough day at work, he used the walking solution. He took a fifteen-minute walk before entering the house. During this walk, he answered three key questions and came up with a three-step to-do list along with explanations and results.

How Does Parasitic Anger Feel?

In the first five minutes of his walk, Dan made himself aware of his physical feelings: his muscular tightness, beating heart, and others. By separating the different physical factors in his aroused state of anger, he found that none were so burdensome that he had to act to rid himself of any one of them.

How Does Parasitic Anger Thinking Sound?

Psychologist Knight Dunlap (1949) observed that when people are asked to describe how they *feel*, they generally respond by describing what they *think*. Dan took Dunlap's advice. In the next five minutes, he took out a notepad, recorded his angry thoughts, and made a connection between his thoughts and his angry feelings. He mainly thought, *I don't get respect.*

What Are the Flaws in Your Thinking?

Dan thought about what it meant if someone didn't act respectfully toward him. He came up with his answer: *You can't win them all.* He next asked himself if he had a hard day at work, how was his family responsible for that? Then he got an insight. What he was thinking about his work had nothing to do with his family. He was bringing his work problems home.

Dan used the fifteen-minute walk to buy time in a different place to think things through. In a little over a week, he started to notice a calming change in his thinking. He entered his home in a slightly better frame of mind.

After three weeks of using the walking solution, Dan no longer rode a raging bull of anger through the door. He walked into his house with a smile and pleasant greeting and found his family happy to see him. The fifteen-minute walk technique was a practical tool that served a limited but important purpose. Dan still had an anger problem related to his work, but for now, he resolved his priority anger problem.

Three Primary Solutions for Anger Escalation: Practical, Empirical, and Core

Your anger can go from barely noticeable to blind rage. How is this variation explained? Sometimes you'll think broadly. Sometimes you'll think parasitically, and your focus will narrow. Your biology influences how you think. For example, poor sleep quality affects your judgments, or you may have a temperamental bent toward anger. Regardless of the causes and reasons for forms and degrees of anger, you can directly dial down parasitic anger at practical, empirical, and core levels. The following describes how.

Practical Solutions

You feel a swell of anger. You think you may be heading for trouble. What are your options? At a *practical level*, you use common-sense techniques that a wise friend may advise, simple techniques supported by science, or approaches that you observe successful and effective people doing advantageously. A friend might suggest taking a walk around the block, getting a cup of coffee at a local coffee joint, counting to 100, or using your cell phone to call a friend to talk things out.

Below are three research-supported practical experiments for you to try. The first experiment puts anger and relaxation into a competition. The second is a longer-term experiment that you can do at your own pace. The third is a thought-counting technique.

SITTING AT THE RIGHT ANGLE

You've probably heard this phrase: "Lean back and relax." Is there anything to it? Sitting at an angle rather than upright can induce relaxation (Krahé, Lutz, and Sylla 2018). You can do this experiment at any time, even right now.

When next you feel stressed and angered, sit back at a thirty-degree angle for five minutes. At the end of that time, does your body feel more relaxed? Test this sitting-back technique five separate times, and use the chart below to record your results. On each of the five trials, check the column that best describes the results you obtained.

More Relaxed	More Stressed or Angry
1.	1.
2.	2.
3.	3.
4.	4.
5.	5.

What did you learn, and how can you use this information to self-improve? Below are examples of what you might have learned.

What I Learned
I noticed less tension in my back. I found that my life goes smoother when I have a relaxing alternative to anger.

Now it's your turn to describe what you learned from your five-trial experiment. Write your responses in the space below.

What I Learned

If sitting at an angle feels calming, here is something you can do at the same time. The next five times you feel a surge of anger, sit back at an angle for five minutes. During that time, create a scene for serenity in your mind where you imagine looking over an open field to a wandering stream. When your body and mind feel relaxed, this can be a good time to make decisions.

NAMING YOUR EMOTION

Understanding your brain will help you employ practical solutions. For example, your amygdala, a small, almond-shaped part of your brain, is a transition point between sensory information from your environment and your emotional responses. In the days before the dawning of thought, language, and emotion, your amygdala was primarily involved in your survival defenses. If your amygdala calculated that your best option was to fight, that's what you would do. However, this is not the same as the emotion of anger. Anger is related to, but not the same as, the automatic fight response.

Your prefrontal cortex is at the center of your cognitive processes of thinking, reasoning, and problem solving. This brain region has connections to your amygdala, the control center for emotions and defense. Both regions switch many emotions on and off, including anger, but do so in different ways.

How can you use this information to benefit yourself? Recognizing when you are angry is a cognitive process. You can use your cognitive capabilities to calm an overly alert and reactive amygdala with a single word: the name of the emotion you are experiencing. This approach can have a calming effect when the emotion is anger. Let's see how this works.

When you name your emotion, or affect, the label originates in your rational brain, trickles down to the amygdala, and reduces anger intensity (Lieberman et al. 2007; Young et al. 2019). Counselors and psychotherapists often encourage people to recognize and name their emotions, also called *affect labeling*. You can encourage yourself to do the same thing.

Over the next week, you are likely to have one or more anger experiences. You can look at this as an opportunity to do an affect labeling experiment. Does naming anger have a detectable calming effect on your amygdala?

The following example shows how to do this experiment. You'll see a column for emotion-activating situations, one for an affect label, and one to record the intensity of your affect after you named your emotion. For this experiment, use either the word "anger" when you feel angry or another anger-related word that best describes your feeling, such as "irritable," "annoyed," or "frustrated."

Situation	Affect Label	Affect Intensity
Cut off in traffic	Anger	Less tense
Misplaced report	Frustration	Less tense
Betrayal: Coworker took my idea without crediting me	Anger	The same

It's your turn to try out affect labeling. Feel free to do this at your own pace. When an anger situation arises, write down the situation, the word that reflects how you feel, and the affect intensity. See if your emotional tone changes and, if so, in what direction it changes.

Situation	Affect Label	Affect Intensity

Does naming your emotion have a calming effect? If so, you have a new tool for helping yourself with anger, one that is simple and convenient to use. If you get mixed results, you've learned when the technique is helpful, when it is not, and when *maybe it's helpful*. That's the beauty of the no-failure approach. The feedback you get is informing.

THE THOUGHT-COUNTING TECHNIQUE

When you feel anger bubbling over, you can count to ten, walk around the block, imagine your positive thoughts combatting your negative ones, or count your aggressive thoughts. Any of the above techniques buy time to lower your risk of acting on aggressive thoughts and impulses. Let's look at the counting technique.

By taking a thought count of nonaggressive and aggressive thoughts, you make yourself aware of what you are thinking and roughly how often. But there is more. When you measure a human process, this normally changes the process because you are observing it. That change can be positive. In this case, counting nonaggressive and aggressive thoughts at predetermined times helps increase nonaggressive thoughts and reduce aggressive thoughts (Kostewicz, Kubina, and Cooper 2000). You may lessen the intensity of aggressive thoughts when you recognize and measure them.

You can use whatever counting system works for you, such as a manual count with a short slash mark for each thought or a tally counter. Tally counters have a button or other means of collecting information on thoughts or actions you want to count. You make a click for each target thought.

Here are a few examples of nonaggressive thoughts: imagining yourself avoiding unnecessary conflicts, imagining yourself helping others think before reacting aggressively, imagining yourself taking responsibility for how you feel, and imagining yourself avoiding a problem when you can see that making a big deal over a small matter isn't worth it. Here are a few aggressive thoughts: *I'll make you suffer*, *You should die*, *I will destroy you*, and *I will hurt you*. Even when you don't act out these thoughts, hostile aggressive thoughts feel unsettling.

Instructions: For four consecutive days, make two recordings of aggressive thoughts and two recordings of nonaggressive thoughts at designated times. Take one minute at each time for the recording. If you have no aggressive thoughts at the time, just record the number zero. (You can increase or decrease the intervals based on your experience.) Here are some suggested times: 9:00 a.m., 1:00 p.m., 4:00 p.m., and 8:00 p.m.

If you've had the same aggressive or nonaggressive thought more than once during the time interval, list the thought once and count each separate incident. Recurring thoughts may be more significant than some of the others.

Use the chart below to record your nonaggressive and aggressive thought results. (You can download blank copies of these thought-counting charts, as well as the chart to note special thoughts, at http://www.newharbinger.com/44321.)

Nonaggressive Thought Sample	Nonaggressive Thought Count
Day 1 9:00: 1:00: 4:00: 8:00:	
Aggressive Thought Sample	**Aggressive Thought Count**
Day 2 9:00: 1:00: 4:00: 8:00:	

Nonaggressive Thought Sample	Nonaggressive Thought Count
Day 3 9:00: 1:00: 4:00: 8:00:	

Aggressive Thought Sample	Aggressive Thought Count
Day 4 9:00: 1:00: 4:00: 8:00:	

If you have aggressive thoughts at a time when you are recording nonaggressive thoughts, and vice versa, tally and record the aggressive thoughts in the following Special Thought Note box. However, aggressive thoughts don't necessarily follow a time schedule. The important thing is to know what you are thinking and to have a rough idea of how often you repeat your nonaggressive and aggressive thoughts.

SPECIAL THOUGHT NOTE	
Nonaggressive Thoughts	**Aggressive Thoughts**

What did you learn from your tally experiment? How can you use this information to self-improve? Here is a sample outcome:

Tally Experiment Learning
What Did I Learn?
When I'm angry, my thoughts are aggressive.
The more I think about my nonaggressive thoughts, the more they surface.
I have fewer angry thoughts when I count nonaggressive thoughts.
How Can I Use This Information?
Recognize that nonaggressive thoughts can extend from anger and support positive actions.
Refocus my thoughts from causing harm to determining a course of action to bring about a favorable result.
Congratulate myself that even when I have aggressive thoughts, I can restrain myself from acting them out.

Now it's your turn to describe what you learned from your tally experiment. Record this information in the space below.

Tally Experiment Learning
What Did I Learn?
How Can I Use This Information?

Temporary solutions can help extinguish a short wick before the flame ignites something bigger. You've consciously recognized a problem and chosen a solution over a reaction. That's a huge advance.

Empirical Solutions

At the *empirical level*, you think like a scientist and test things out. A scientist might change a factor and see if the results are any different. That's part of the experimental method.

Let's say that a neighbor is playing loud music after 10:00 p.m., and you have trouble hearing your TV over the sound. You feel anger. The question is, why? The obvious answer is that the music is the cause, or the damn neighbor is the cause. There is a point to that view. Without the noise, would you have responded angrily? However, there is more to the situation when you view the situation through the lens of a scientific thinker.

When you decide to think scientifically, you start by asking yourself three questions: (1) What am I telling myself about the situation? (2) What am I telling myself about my feelings? (3) What actions do I "feel" like taking?

In the following chart, you can see how this empirical approach plays out using the neighbor's loud music example. Column one is a sampling of parasitic anger approaches, column two is a coping approach, and column three is a possible outcome.

Parasitic Anger Approach	Alternative Coping Approach	Possible Outcome of Alternative Coping Approach
What am I telling myself? *This noise shouldn't be.*	Accept that what is, is, not what you think it should be. In this case, acceptance does not mean acquiescence. Rather, it is an acknowledgment of a fact. Ask yourself where this event ranks in importance in your life. In this case, the music is not a big issue in your life. It is more like a gnat bite. Nevertheless, this is still annoying but not the same as the world ending in a ball of fire.	You feel annoyed with the loud music, but you no longer have a strong urge to get back at your neighbor by blasting your music.
What am I telling myself about my feelings? *I can't stand it.*	Ask yourself why you can't stand what you don't like. The reality is that you are tolerating what you don't like. However, by defining a situation as intolerable, it becomes what you think.	Your stress level goes down to a normal level despite a change in your environment that you find aversive. You no longer define it as intolerable.
What actions do I feel like taking? *I'll turn my speakers toward the neighbor's residence and blast louder music.*	You approach your neighbor and calmly ask him to turn down the volume.	You discover that your neighbor is out of town and his teenage son is blaring the music. The teen turns off the music.

It is your turn to experiment. Describe your own parasitic process. Test a coping approach. Record your results.

Parasitic Anger Approach	Alternative Coping Approach	Possible Outcome of Alternative Coping Approach

By putting a spotlight on a problem, you may see it in a different light.

Core Solutions

At a *core level*, you explore what is behind your parasitic anger patterns. Here are eight sample core issues along with sample core solutions:

Core Issue: Having a stronger tendency toward anger than most

Core Solution: Be mindful of that tendency and step back more often to reflect to avoid needless anger crises.

Core Issue: Believing that you are powerful when you're angry and intimidating, and weak when you're not, and therefore going out of your way to show you are tough

Core Solution: Explore how to develop mental toughness through tolerance.

Core Issue: Having a short trigger for anger when you are in a bad mood or feel depressed

Core Solution: Use that anger signal to work on overcoming depression.

Core Issue: Having grown up in a family or community that blamed others for their troubles and finding you often do the same

Core Solution: Find ways to break that family tradition and set a positive new one.

Core Issue: Having cynical beliefs, such as that you can't trust anybody, and automatically looking for proof of this belief

Core Solution: Figure out what information you need, on a case-by-case basis, for deciding who merits the benefit of the doubt and whom you'd wisely not trust.

Core Issue: Having a sense of entitlement to whatever you want, possibly basing your worth on succeeding, and angrily kicking back when you don't get your way

Core Solution: Learn to think outside of this all-or-nothing view to help yourself forge a happier and healthier perspective.

Core Issue: Believing that no one should dare challenge you, and absorbing yourself too much in the importance of your views

Core Solution: Add flexibility to your life by accepting that others have a right to their views, even if misguided.

Core Issue: Having low tolerance for tension (being easily set off)

Core Solution: Develop methods of building a higher tolerance for tension.

Write down three priority core issues that merit your attention and your tentative core solutions.

Core Issues	Core Solutions
1.	
2.	
3.	

Keep an eraser handy. You may alter this priority list with new information.

MY PROGRESS LOG

Together we will cover a lot of ground in this book. Unless you have a photographic memory, you'll forget a lot. Logging is a tested way to keep track of important ideas and to have a direct way to access them later. You'll find a progress log at the end of each chapter to record what you found useful and how you used the information.

Your progress log has five sections: key ideas, action plan, execution, results, and revisions.

Key ideas: What three ideas did you pick up from this chapter that you found most helpful?

1.

2.

3.

Action plan: What three steps would you take to move closer to overcoming anger excesses?

1.

2.

3.

Execution: What are you going to do to execute the steps? (The process)

1.

2.

3.

Results: What do you hope to learn—or have reinforced—by taking these steps?

1.

2.

3.

Revisions: If you would make changes in the process, what would you do differently next time?

1.

2.

3.

Over the past thirty years, I have found that those who actively (begrudgingly, acceptingly, or enthusiastically) tested ideas were considerably more likely to start doing better sooner. I also found that no two people highlighted the same ideas. All were different. But isn't that the way it is? Some like strawberry ice cream, some like chocolate, and some prefer cookies or pie.

CHAPTER 2

Six Ways to Combat Anger

Put on your experimenter's hat, and let's look at six ways to combat parasitic anger. In this chapter, we'll cover

- how to overcome a harmful anger cycle;

- why expelling tension from anger through cathartic yelling and throwing things reinforces the tendency to feel angry;

- how to bring the excesses out of parasitic forms of blame and escape the blame trap;

- how to avoid what is called "fundamental attribution errors";

- the importance of appraising a situation (or person) from different angles to avoid jumping to conclusions, to read things accurately, and to experience less needless anger;

- how adopting a philosophy of acceptance helps you better tolerate aversive situations, be in command of yourself, and improve your ability to respond proportionately; and

- why, when you pursue your enlightened self-interest, you'll have fewer needless anger episodes.

Before we delve into the six anger-combatting strategies, it's important to understand what a harmful anger cycle is.

RECOGNIZING A HARMFUL ANGER CYCLE

Reducing or ridding yourself of parasitic beliefs starts with becoming aware of these thinking traps. A parasitic form of anger is a cyclical process triggered by undesired events and colored by negative, irrational beliefs, with the power to stimulate emotional arousal and behavioral responses including aggression. (See the cognitive behavioral anger cycle on the next page.)

You can take charge of yourself to change the process and break the cycle by guiding your reason to achieve that end. The strategies you learn in this chapter will help you do that.

ANGER-COMBATTING APPROACHES

Among the following six approaches, invest your time and energy in the one that works best for you.

Break Free from Catharsis

In the classic 1976 movie *Network*, we hear *"angry man"* TV newscaster Howard Beale venting, "I don't have to tell you that things are bad… Punks are running wild in the street… We know the air is unfit to breathe and our food is unfit to eat…" When he finishes his gripes, Beale asks his audience to stick their heads out the window and yell, "I am as mad as hell, and I'm not going to take this anymore!" Beale's solution is a catharsis solution.

Catharsis is a common anger solution. You act to relieve yourself of anger tensions by pounding pillows, slamming doors, throwing dishes, screaming, and ranting and raving. Is this an effective way to defeat needless anger? Some off-the-beaten-path therapy systems involve screaming—and lots of it. Psychiatrist Dan Casriel (1974), author of *A Scream Away from Happiness*, created a system where people screamed to release tension. There is no meaningful evidence for that approach.

California psychiatrist Arthur Janov's (1975) primal scream therapy is a pseudoscience system that lacks empirical support but may have a short-term placebo effect for some. Some of Janov's beliefs are unconventional and controversial, such as that primal pain can start before or just at birth and that screaming about these experiences can be curative. Other than the author's descriptions of effectiveness, primal scream therapy floats untethered in an ethereal world.

Most people—even those with normally calm temperaments—occasionally vent. This is hardly fatal. Venting, however, is different from expressing feelings, such as saying, "I feel sad" or "I felt angry when you acted dismissively toward me." Emotional expression is typically healthy. In contrast, discharging tension by kicking and screaming is temper-tantrum stuff that you can dignify by the word "catharsis." Unfortunately, anger catharsis normally does more long-term harm than good (Bushman 2002). Instead of relief, you might feel riled up and worse for a longer time. Catharsis is rarely an answer for anger. However, it's better to scream or hit a wall than kick a pet, beat a child, or get into physical fights.

Try a different way to discharge anger tensions, such as exercise. After even thirty minutes of exercise, more oxygenated blood goes to the brain for a few hours. You are likely to think with greater clarity about matters you want to resolve.

Different provocative situations take different approaches for discharging tension resulting from anger. Sometimes a strong assertion is reasonable. At other times, listening before acting makes sense. Altering changeable parts of an environment, as well as removing yourself from a toxic setting, can be effective. And sometimes your response would best be directed to defuse your anger-evoking parasitic beliefs. Here, the idea is not to find a middle ground but rather to find ways to overthrow a dysfunctional parasitic belief(s).

Escape the Blame Trap

We live in a blame culture nested in an age of anger. Blame and anger, like the air, are everywhere. Although holding people responsible for their actions is socially functional, blame excesses, extensions, and exonerations are typically problematic (Knaus 2000). You'll commonly find these big three blame factors in parasitic anger patterns:

- **Blame excesses:** These include faultfinding, nitpicking, and complaining. You put on your defect-detection glasses, identify a defect or mistake in another person, and see yourself as justified in blaming the person and angering yourself over what the person does that displeases you.

- **Extensions of blame:** You extend blame when you demean, put down, or damn yourself, others, or life. These extensions of blame include dehumanizing and depersonalizing others, such as declaring the targeted person(s) a scumbag, idiot, bitch, bastard, creep, and more. When you degrade others, you believe that you are superior and have the right to harm them. Extensions of blame are a major anger-generating force.

- **Blame exonerations:** These are defenses against blame. Most people prefer to maintain a good reputation and positive public image. Blame affects how people think of you (ten Brinke, Vohs, and Carney 2016), so you engage in ego-preserving defenses that include rationalizations, denials, and deflections.

Here is a classic example of extension of blame: The Nevada Supreme Court removed juvenile court judge Deacon Jones for improper conduct, which included the use of extreme and threatening language. Briefly, the case involved the following: Deacon Jones had created a squabble with another judge, Jane Prochaska. The problem started when Jones accused Prochaska of being derelict in her duties. Jones, figuratively, made a federal case of something that was probably none of his business. According to court records: "Jones spoke of putting dynamite in the tailpipe of Prochaska's car and of burying Prochaska in the sand up to her head, pouring honey over her head, and putting ants on her head" (Gray 2002, 126). Jones justified his actions by calling Prochaska a "[expletive deleted] bitch." Presumably, Jones's arbitrary description of Prochaska's character justified the atrocities he had in mind. But the Supreme Court justices had a different view, and Jones lost his position.

Avoid Fundamental Attribution Errors

Parasitic anger, like parasitic anxiety, depression, and so on, has a distinctive pattern of thought called a *cognitive signature*. A cognitive signature is a predictable line of thought that goes with anger, anxiety, depressive conditions, and more. For example, a common cognitive signature for depression is helplessness and hopelessness. Anxiety's signature includes anticipation of threat and powerlessness to cope. Parasitic anger's signatures are varied and include hostile thoughts such as, *If you don't give me what I want, I'm going to hurt you*; *I should get my way, or there will be hell to pay*; and *I hate you, and I'll destroy you.*

Parasitic cognitive signatures repeatedly lead to negative outcomes. So, why not change them when you experience them? Let's consider an example. Jill acted badly toward Jack by joking about him in front of his friends. What do you think? If you think Jill is a witch, that is your *attribution*. Would you blame Jack for calling Jill a witch? What if you learned that Jack previously berated Jill for her hairstyle in front of her friends? Would you think that Jack was a hypocrite? Would you consider Jill's response fair "payback"?

"Witch" and "hypocrite" are character generalizations that represent *fundamental attribution errors*. You make a fundamental attribution error when you, the observer, jump to a conclusion and heap blame on others based on your judgment of their character. You could just as easily disagree with their choices. Here are some common fundamental attribution errors:

- A child won't share a toy. That makes the child a *selfish imp*.

- A bank clerk miscounts the money, and the error is in the bank's favor. You think bank clerks are the real *bank robbers*.

- Someone talks too loudly at a restaurant. You think of the person as an *inconsiderate jerk*.

Once you've degraded the person, you can justify retribution. However, let's flip things around. What if you are the one who talked too loudly, or told someone not to do something and then did it yourself, or made a calculation error? If you made a calculation error, you are likely to see this as situational. Maybe someone distracted you. You lacked information. You were too stressed to think straight. People should understand you're not perfect. You exonerate yourself from blame and move on.

Anger attribution errors typically involve character generalizations, extensions of blame, and justifications for punishing. By flipping things around, you might develop empathy for another's foibles and faults in a situation and help yourself break an extension-of-blame habit. Empathy, or feeling understanding for another's situation (putting yourself in the other's shoes), is incompatible with extension-of-blame thinking.

The following are examples of how anger attributions involving extensions of blame can look in situations when you are the "observer" and in situations where you are the "actor."

- **Observer:** You are in a hurry to get to the airport, and you get behind a driver in the passing lane going at the speed limit. You slow down. You can't get around the driver. You think, *The guy's a selfish jerk. He's trying to slow everyone down.* You wish you had a 20 mm cannon mounted on the hood of your car. You think, *That would take care of the SOB.* If you had any doubts about how you felt, this extension-of-blame thinking is a parasitic angry way of thinking.

- **Actor:** While driving at the speed limit in the passing lane, you are thinking about a sick friend in the hospital. You're not watching your speedometer and are driving a little too slowly. The driver behind you starts honking and flipping you the bird. You might believe the other driver did not give you the benefit of the doubt, instead thinking you were intentionally slowing down traffic.

Here is a comparison of these two views.

Extension-of-Blame View	Personal Situation View
You think the action is intentional (and thus blamable and condemnable).	You see the matter as situational (and thus understandable and forgivable).
You think the act reflects the person's character or disposition (and is thus blamable and condemnable).	You think the act is explainable by what happened to cause the event and is therefore understandable and forgivable.

Next time you anger yourself over a stranger's behavior, try a comparison exercise. Compare the character generalizations you might make of another's actions with how you would like others to view you in a similar circumstance.

Extension-of-Blame View	Personal Situation View

What did you discover from the experiment that you can use to support future reappraisals? For your record, write it below.

Reappraise Situations

You are walking on a crowded city sidewalk, and you feel someone bump you as you pass. You think this was intentional, and your anger feelings rise. Situations like this, where you jump to a conclusion, are opportunities to practice *cognitive reappraisal*. Cognitive reappraisal is a technique for taking a second look at a situation to see if you can amend its meaning and wring out the excesses. The idea is not to fool yourself into believing something fake, but rather to honestly see a situation as realistically as you can at the time.

The method is useful in parasitic anger situations. Let's use the bumping example. You've judged the event. You feel gnarled inside. Fortunately, you've learned that reappraisals can result in a reduction in angry feelings (Takebe, Takahashi, and Sato 2017), calm a reactive amygdala (Buhle et al. 2014), and yield added benefits as a distancing technique (Picó-Pérez et al. 2019). You decide to give cognitive reappraisal a try. You start by asking yourself, *How might I view this situation differently?* Here is a reappraisal: *The person wasn't paying attention.* This new view is plausible.

You can start developing reappraisal skills using *guided reappraisals*. In the example below, in the left column, you'll find questions and sample situations where you can apply the questions. The middle column shows a way of looking at the situation from a different angle. The column on the right is for describing the results of the reappraisal strategy.

Reappraisal Strategy	Reappraisal Strategy Questions	Results
What's my price? Try this in situations where you don't think you can stand the tension.	If someone offered me $10,000 for each minute I hung in with feeling stressed until the stress lessened, how much could I earn?	I still don't like feeling tense, but tension seems much more tolerable.

Reappraisal Strategy	Reappraisal Strategy Questions	Results
What if this were my favorite cousin? Consider having to wait for an acquaintance at lunchtime, and feeling angry. Try viewing the acquaintance as your favorite cousin.	Would I think differently if this were my favorite, but absent-minded, cousin? What can I take from the analysis and application to the current situation? Would I be more forgiving?	Perhaps the acquaintance forgot, got delayed, was without a cell phone, or was in an accident. I still don't like the situation, but I feel calmer.
What's my anger angle? Try this in situations where your anger might get out of hand.	What can I tell myself to cool this anger down a few degrees? Note: This experiment is about monitoring your thinking. In chapter 3, you'll learn more about stripping away irrational factors in parasitic anger.	I start with measuring the event on an *importance scale*, where 1 is a "shrug your shoulders" and 10 is devastating. I ask myself, *Where does the situation lie on the importance scale?* The situation was a 3. I stopped acting like this was a 10+.
How can I look at this from another's perspective? Try this in situations where you are going overboard and prefer to regain perspective.	If a wise friend was in the situation representing my interests, how might that friend see and do things differently?	The friend would address the issue directly and honestly at the level warranted.
What is my view from different camera angles? Try this in situations when your anger thoughts are accelerating in a conflict situation.	Situations can look different when viewed from different angles. Imagine yourself in a room with multiple computer screens, each showing an area from different camera angles. You get new information from each angle. Here are five angles: (1) What are the likely thoughts of the other person? (2) What can I agree to do? (3) What is negotiable? (4) Where do I need to hold my ground? (5) What is the worst thing that can happen if I walk away to revisit this matter at another time?	By getting new angles on a situation, I have more options for better decision making.

Reapprisal Strategy	Reappraisal Strategy Questions	Results
What changes with space and time distancing? Try this in situations when you realize you are too close to a stress situation and risk losing your objectivity.	Is it possible to imagine yourself 1,000 miles away from the stress event and reading about the event in last week's newspaper? If every sentence in the article contained objective observations and facts, what might a reader say about the event 200 years from now? When you create conditions to get distance from excess negativity, you are likely to think more clearheadedly.	I found I could create an accurate statement of the situation and delete the expletives, impressions, and beliefs that cluttered my mind. I concluded that the situation hardly warranted the anger and distress I was giving it. The situation would be a non-event 200 years hence. I felt in command of myself, and that felt damned good.

You can apply cognitive reappraisal and distancing methods to reduce parasitic anger and improve your outlook. However, context is important. Think of it like a job. If you avoid improving your work performance, cognitive reappraisal, as a stand-alone intervention, is insufficient. Doing better on the job is likely to earn you an improved job appraisal (Troy, Shallcross, and Mauss 2013).

Let's apply what you've learned to your own cognitive reappraisal experiment.

MY COGNITIVE REAPPRAISAL EXPERIMENT

Without an initial appraisal that evoked anger, there would be no need for a reappraisal. By testing a variety of reappraisal approaches, you can expect to find some that work better for you than others.

What you learn through reappraising may lead to more effective first appraisals.

Reapprisal Strategy	Reappraisal Question Strategy	Results
What's my price?		

What if this were my favorite cousin?		
What's my anger angle?		
How can I look at this from another's perspective?		
What is my view from different camera angles?		
What changes with space and time distancing?		

By developing reappraisal skills, you are also teaching yourself how to substitute parasitic anger appraisals with more accurate initial appraisals. Reappraisals can have additional benefits, such as improving your chances for long-term physical and psychological health (Zaehringer et al. 2018), lessening tension that goes with a sense of uncontrollability (King and dela Rosa 2019), navigating uncontrollable stresses while avoiding destructive mental health outcomes (Troy and Mauss 2011), and maintaining the effectiveness you've earned in developing reappraisal skills (Denny and Ochsner 2014).

The following top tip will give you an important new way to use the cognitive reappraisal method. As you'll see, this tip ties into the anger cycle, which we discussed at the beginning of the chapter.

Top Tip: Step Back and Distance Yourself from Your Anger

Stefan G. Hofmann is a professor of psychology in the Department of Psychological and Brain Sciences, Boston University. As an expert in CBT and the author of *The Anxiety Skills Workbook* (Hofmann 2020), he shares his top tip for distancing yourself from anger.

Anger is a normal human emotion that can arise from experiencing frustration or a violation of one's personal space or norms. You can focus anger on a person, including yourself, or an object, and it can be a general experience. You can experience anger at varying levels of physiological arousal.

Anger can range from short-lasting rage to long-lasting resentment. Rage often has a sudden onset and is associated with the perception of loss of control. Regardless of the type of anger, there is always (1) a stimulus triggering it, (2) cognitive appraisal that makes the stimulus personally meaningful, and (3) a time course of the emotional response. Once you know the cycle, you know where you can intervene to break the pattern. Here's how:

1. *Step back from your immediate response to the stimulus.* Is the stimulus that important to you? Is it as personally relevant as you first assumed it to be?

2. *Step back from your immediate appraisal of the situation.* Is it possible that your immediate appraisal of the situation was incorrect? Is it possible that somebody violated your space or norms unintentionally? Are there any contributing factors that might explain or even justify the other person's behavior?

3. *Step back from your emotional response.* You are not your feeling. You are not the puppet of your emotions. Distance yourself from your emotions by observing yourself and your response. Nobody forces you to respond to your feelings. You may not have control over your emotional arousal, but you do have control over your behavior—what you say or do. Consider the consequences of your actions.

Try Three Dimensions of Acceptance

You might want and expect everyone to act fairly toward you. You might expect yourself to act with perfect judgment. So, what do you make of it when you get the opposite of what you expect? You might join the Deacon Jones Fan Club and conjure atrocities in your mind to strike back in fantasy, if not in actuality. When you are inclined to go in that direction, is it possible to try another way?

Psychologist Albert Ellis's three dimensions of acceptance are an alternative to the harsh world of extension-of-blame thinking and parasitic anger. The three acceptances are to accept yourself, others, and life unconditionally.

Unconditional acceptance is a philosophy and, thus, a choice. It's not an easy choice as acceptance takes time and practice. Here is the core principle for acceptance: *Things are as they are, and not necessarily as you might always like or expect them to be.*

If you think unconditional acceptance merits exploring, here are some points to consider:

- Acceptance is not the same as passive acquiescence. If someone treats you unfairly, you can accept that this has happened because it happened. You can assertively change what you can, accept the unchangeable, and compensate as best you can when your options are less than ideal.

- Acceptance and awareness often fuse in present-moment situations. You are open to your experiences. You pursue experiences you like. You don't have to like all that you experience.

- Acceptance is not an *anything goes* philosophy. You don't have a license to do anything you want because "I can unconditionally accept myself." Self-acceptance is not a right to act irresponsibly.

- Acceptance includes judging without being judgmental. Acceptance involves acting in a socially and personally responsible way. Acceptance includes believing that you are not responsible for your tendencies toward anger, but you are responsible for overcoming excess anger.

- The language of acceptance is moderate but accurate. An unpleasant event is an unpleasant event. You think in words like "prefer" (not "must have") and "inconvenient" (not "horrible"). Moderate language ("prefer") prompts a clearer perspective. Harsh language ("must have," "horrible") is likely to stir up your amygdala.

- Unconditional acceptance reduces the risk of creating secondary problems, like layering a problem onto a problem. These secondary problems include blaming yourself, blaming others, and blaming the world because you can't control what happened or how you feel.

- Acceptance is associated with fewer negative emotions in stressful circumstances (Ford et al. 2018).

Acceptance philosophies invariably clash with extension-of-blame views. You can't logically be extending blame and having thoughts to harm someone while accepting unpleasant situations as they are.

MY ACCEPTANCE EXERCISE

In the following chart, compare extension-of-blame, situational, and acceptance views and see what you learn. The first row is an example. Here's the situation: A flight attendant brought you lukewarm coffee; you wanted hot coffee. You fill in the remaining blanks with examples of your own.

Extension-of-Blame View	Situational Explanation View	Acceptance View	What I Learned from the Comparison
The dumb flight attendant brought me cool coffee!	There are too many passengers to the number of flight attendants.	What is out of the control of the flight attendant is a shared concern for me. Cool coffee is better than no coffee.	In this situation, I found that I have many reasonable ways to view a situation.

What did you discover from this experiment that you can use to support future reappraisals? For your record, write it below.

Pursue Enlightened Self-Interest

Enlightened self-interest is a philosophy for advancing and actualizing yourself without needlessly harming others. Without expecting reciprocity, you might selectively further the interests of others when you don't harm yourself in the process.

It's normally in your enlightened self-interest to work fairly with others, earn trust, and boost your opportunities for cooperation where all benefit from a joint effort. While desirable, reciprocity (i.e., others acting the same way toward you) is not a requirement.

When you don't expect others to conform to your expectations, but still hold them accountable for negative actions, you move yourself outside of the parasitic anger cycle. That is in your enlightened self-interest.

MY PROGRESS LOG

Key ideas: What three ideas did you pick up from this chapter that you found most helpful?

1.

2.

3.

Action plan: What three steps would you take to move closer to overcoming anger excesses?

1.

2.

3.

Execution: What are you going to do to execute the steps (the process)?

1.

2.

3.

Results: What do you hope to learn—or have reinforced—by taking these steps?

1.

2.

3.

Revisions: If you would make changes in the process, what would you do differently next time?

1.

2.

3.

Pathways to Positive Change

If you are like practically everyone else, you have parasitic anger blind spots. How can you know? You repeat patterns with the same poor results. For example, when you repeatedly feel riled over social situations and act as if the situations exclusively caused the feeling, that's a blind spot.

Paul Dubois, the founder of rational therapy, asserted that emotional thinking is a blind spot for many. He wrote, "Let us note the fact that if the conduct of others has been the cause of our emotions, it is really we ourselves who have created it by the way we have reacted" (Dubois 1909a, 155).

The more you know about your parasitic anger thoughts, the quicker you can spot them and rid yourself of them. In this chapter, we'll explore four ways to free yourself from the harmful feelings that arise from parasitic anger thinking so that you can more happily and realistically get on with your life. These methods, briefly, involve

- discarding false parasitic beliefs to start on the path to emotional freedom;

- learning and using Albert Ellis's famous ABCDE technique to hone your reasoning skills to set yourself free from the inner tyranny of parasitic anger thinking; and

- promoting mental flexibility and tolerance for reality by substituting probability thinking rules for black-and-white, absolutist parasitic thinking.

With fewer parasitic anger patterns to contend with, the chances are that you'll experience harmony between what you think, feel, and do.

THE POWER OF BELIEFS

You are a part of a belief-making species. Your core beliefs represent your convictions for what is true and false, right and wrong. Your beliefs are fused with the meaning you give to your life, to things, and to why people do what they do. Your beliefs influence whether you'll tend to view situations on a scale, as probabilities, or in black-and-white terms. Some will be fact-based beliefs, some will contain partial truths, and some will be fuzzy or false.

Of course, you'll evaluate, judge, and organize your actions through combinations of cognitive processes, such as logic, reason, intuition, insight, heuristics (rules of thumb), associations from experience, "common sense," and so on. Nevertheless, your beliefs often color those processes as well as your perceptions and perspectives.

Beliefs will range in strength from firm convictions that are impervious to disconfirming facts to loosely held views from something you heard. You'll naturally ground some of your beliefs in experience. For example, you believe your best friends have high integrity because they routinely keep commitments and act responsibly.

You may believe your future will be positive and you'll find a way to meet challenges, both those that you anticipate and those that are still unknown. Even if this is a misguided belief, the odds are you'll lead a healthier, happier life than a person with a pessimistic belief that one bad thing after another is looming in the future.

Some beliefs are implausible. You think others should play by your rules (as if they do not have rules of their own), and you anger yourself when they don't. If you act as if you believe that another's worth depends on what you think of them, that's a fallacy. Here is a test for the strength of your conviction: What are you willing to bet that no one can contest that belief convincingly, including you?

A *New York Post* journalist reputedly asked the famous philosopher Bertrand Russell "if he was willing to die for his beliefs. 'Of course not,' he replied. 'After all, I may be wrong'" (*New York Post*, June 23, 1964).

Beliefs are not equal. Believing in the tooth fairy as a child is different from believing as an adult that people who disagree with you deserve wrathful vengeance. Beliefs also come in distinct forms.

One form is *metacognitive beliefs*, or beliefs about your thoughts, such as that negative thoughts are uncontrollable. Metacognitive beliefs about not being able to control negative thoughts tend to reinforce the very same negative thoughts that the thinker wants to stop (Caselli et al. 2017). This is unfortunate because beliefs that you can't control your thoughts tend to activate anxiety (Melli et al. 2017).

The issue isn't whether you can stop the flow of thoughts. Your stream of consciousness is ongoing. You can think about your thinking, and to one degree or another, you can redirect your flow in rational, positive ways and debunk harmful fictions and fallacies. Cognitive reappraisal is an example. In the "ABCDE Process" section that follows, you'll learn how to use another research-supported approach to do the same thing.

Some beliefs are fact-based and rational, such as that water is necessary for life, regular dental care reduces your risk of a heart attack, and the sun will rise in the east. Because you can prove them, they are *fact-based beliefs*, or *truths*. Who would bet against them?

Some beliefs are irrational (inconsistent with observation, fact, or reality). For example, an irrational belief is that for you to be a happy person, you must be free of all tension forever. Another is that people who violate your beliefs, rules, and role expectations are rotten to the core and deserve the worst. These beliefs are as valid as believing that bald eagles and rabbits are natural friends. However, when you experience them as incontestable truths, you'll feel and act per your beliefs in situations that activate them.

Are your core beliefs powerful? In the Pacific Ocean theater, near the end of World War II, Japanese authorities sent young pilots to fly into vessels in the US fleet. Our primal instincts are to survive and thrive. This suicide run went against that mandate. Yet close to 4,000 pilots flew to their deaths on kamikaze bombing runs. What makes this a complex issue? The pilots learned that they would fly on a divine wind to heaven for their heroic deeds of saving the Japanese nation, as the winds had saved the nation centuries before. The narrative fits with history and strong tradition to not surrender but to die honorably. When the commanders asked for volunteers, they did so in a group setting where backing off would be an act of dishonor and shame, which was also rooted in the Japanese culture. History, tradition, and the power of group conformity overwhelmed the survival instinct.

Top Tip: Uncovering Anger Beliefs

Situations can trigger beliefs that ignite emotions, such as parasitic anger. Jimmy Walter, a philanthropist and a student of reason, talks about making the connection between situations, beliefs, and emotions.

The baseball game ends with a 1 to 0 score. The fans of both teams show emotions such as joy, disappointment, or anger. Ask fans why they feel as they do, and you'll hear something about the game, such as the score.

Most people believe that situations cause emotions. However, different emotions about the same score in a game show that the event isn't the only factor triggering the emotion.

Why is the belief that links the situation and feeling often hard to see? You don't pay attention to your thinking. How do you find the beliefs in the feelings if you don't, at first, see them? Search for the belief. If your favorite team lost and you feel mad, you might hear yourself say something like, *The other team cheated, and the manager should boil in oil.* That's your angry thought.

Of course, there are exceptions, such as natural anger when you are physically attacked, or sadness and grief over the loss of a loved one. But these are a tiny percentage of events. You can exaggerate them, and that's a danger, too. So, look for exaggerations. When you bring them out of the shadows, you'll find a core source of human misery.

THE ABCDE PROCESS

For over six decades, hundreds of thousands of self-helpers have used Albert Ellis's rational emotive behavior therapy (REBT) techniques. His ABCDE approach to positive change is the centerpiece for most CBT systems. Over fifty years of research affirm the effectiveness of REBT (David et al. 2018). REBT is an important tool to reduce cognitive forms of harmful anger and promote positive emotions (Oltean et al. 2018).

Understanding the Acronym

In the ABCDE acronym, each letter stands for a different phase of a positive, highly structured change process. Here's how it works.

A = Activating events. *Activating events* are situations with the power to trigger emotions and actions. They can be pleasant, such as seeing an old friend, or unpleasant, such as being yelled at by your boss. If you feel a wave of natural anger, that means a threat is near and attack may be your safest choice.

With parasitic anger, you rightly or wrongly view the event as aversive and automatically default to negative, inciting thoughts. Based on how much you make of the situation, your aroused anger will range in magnitude from minor to severe. Because anger occurs in degrees, you already have the power to exercise some control over your anger reactions. That's a cause for optimism.

Many events can trigger parasitic anger. However, whether you respond parasitically depends on the meaning that you give to the situation. You'll likely take situational factors into account. If an inebriated and disoriented person started cursing loudly at you, would you shrug it off, figuring you can't expect a drunk to act sober? Would you angrily yell back? What you might do gets us to point B, your beliefs.

B = Beliefs. You'll filter many emotive-type experiences through *beliefs*. The beliefs mediate (provoke, trigger, activate, amplify) how you feel. Some will be plausible, reasonable, logical, or fact-based. These are your rational beliefs. However, biased, distorted, irrational beliefs are part of human nature, too. They are normally automatic and thus quickly activated. These presumed truths lack proof and are unjustifiable. That's what makes them irrational.

Not all irrational beliefs are harmful. You believe that throwing salt over your left shoulder will knock down an evil spirit sitting on your shoulder and bring you good luck. The belief is irrational. When it has no meaningful effect on your life, it's no big deal. However, anger aroused from an irrational belief practically always has a parasitic part. Here are a few examples: you act as if you believe impositions and inconveniences are intolerable; you need to have what you want when you want it; people must approve of you regardless of what you do. If a person violates these conditions, the same irrational thoughts will surface, and your anger temperature will ordinarily rise.

There is more. Cognitive forms of anger often involve externalizing blame (i.e., blaming other people, things, or situations): "A barking dog made me angry"; "My mate hassled me about drinking, and that made me angry"; "It's a cloudy day, and that makes me angry." This *reflex theory* of anger is easy to falsify. Do you believe that you have no choice but to feel angry if, say, it's a cloudy day? What if you were a farmer looking forward to the rain during a drought?

C = Consequences. *Consequences* are the emotional and behavioral results that follow from what you believe about an activating event. If you view life through rational lenses, you'll have normal negative feelings in response to adversity that may include some degree of anger when dealing with issues such as deceptions and unfairness. However, as parasitic anger (irrational) scripts play out, negative consequences are likely to follow. Here are six examples of possible consequences extending from irrational, parasitic anger beliefs:

- Episodes of physical (yelling, fighting) or indirect (gossiping, backstabbing) aggression that boomerang in the form of retaliation

- An anger cycle that triggers more anger thinking and feelings

- Deteriorating quality of interpersonal relationships

- Lingering, visceral memories of anger experiences that are too late to resolve

- Repeating undesirable anger effects because you've overpracticed your anger scripts

- Periods of feeling distressed when you don't want to feel that way

The previous consequences occur in degrees and often in combinations. Sometimes you won't have meaningful consequences for brief, controlled, infrequent parasitic anger episodes, and sometimes a single event can prove disastrous.

D = Dispute. *Dispute* means to question and challenge irrational beliefs that stimulate negative emotions and behavioral outcomes. By separating parasitic (irrational) beliefs from factual beliefs, you've already made a start in this process. If you work with an REBT therapist or read multiple REBT books, you'll find many examples for recognizing and disputing erroneous beliefs. For a start, you might benefit from using a guided approach of asking and answering the following four questions when you are angering yourself and suspect you're thinking parasitically:

1. If twelve people observed the same event that you believe triggers your anger, would they all come to the same conclusion? By asking this question, you've paused to consider alternative appraisals.

2. What part of my anger thinking is likely to be rational, verifiable, or factual? At this point, you are looking for evidence and proof.

3. What part of my anger thinking is likely to be parasitic (irrational)? Recognizing this thinking, and knowing it is changeable, can bring relief.

4. Does the belief(s) I hold about this situation advance or detract from achieving constructive goals? This question can lead to focusing your attention on your priorities rather than on distractions or fictional problems.

E = Effects. New *effects* come from your efforts to examine your thinking, test new behaviors, and generate a fresh perspective, which is a common by-product of purging the parasites from your thinking. With fewer unreasoned expectations, extension-of-blame beliefs, or questionable assumptions, you'll spend less time in vicious anger cycles. You may experience improved relationships with others as they view you as more tolerant.

Let's look at an ABCDE example and see how to work this system.

Putting the ABCDE Process into Action

Pat, one of your coworkers, walked by you in a hall without greeting you. You feel angry. You believe that Pat ignored you to insult you. You blame Pat for being (not acting but being) petty and uncivil. You extend blame by telling yourself that Pat is a rotten human being, and it is your right to punish Pat for this lousy attitude. You quickly experience the angry feeling that results from these thoughts.

Using the Pat example, let's look at how to organize your information the ABCDE way.

Activating event. Factual observations are activating events. Pat walked past you in the hall without greeting you.

Beliefs. You may overlook your beliefs by putting your attention on the evocative event. After all, how many people believe that they are making assumptions and acting on beliefs while they are in the process of doing this? Here is a straightforward question for tuning into your beliefs when you are in an angry state of mind: *What do I believe about the event?* If you know what you are telling yourself (what you believe), you can check the validity of the belief. What are you telling yourself about Pat? Is it that Pat shouldn't snub you? Do you think Pat is a rotten person for snubbing you or just rotten in general? Do you have an urge to punish Pat for being a rotten person? Are you the person to make this happen? This type of analysis can surface parasitic thoughts and the negative anger feelings and behavioral consequences that so often go with them.

Consequences. Here is what is going on. Pat walked past you. You almost instantly felt angry. That's the emotional consequence, or C. You may want to call Pat out. That's a potential behavioral consequence that may or may not pan out well. Here a lot depends on your approach and whether your belief is true or false. Probe a little deeper, and you may see a consequence that is more about you than Pat. You may tune into a vicious circle of angry thoughts → angry feelings → angry thoughts. Do you want to live with these preventable consequences, or try a different way? Let's try a different way.

Dispute. If you think Pat *made* you angry, does this mean that Pat is the author of the anger scripts in your mind? Does Pat have telepathy and the ability to control your thoughts and force you to feel angry? If this is starting to sound silly, it is as it sounds. You can blame it on Pat, but where does that get you? If you've gotten this far in the process, you are on your way to doing an instant retake of the situation. You evaluate your thoughts and stick to rational ways of thinking and doing. You can do this without changing a thing about Pat.

Throughout the book, you'll find many ways to dispute parasitic thinking. For now, let's start with the four basic questions that can promote clarity and reduce needless anger. You'll see them in column one of the following chart. Column two suggests plausible, rational answers.

Four Standard Questions	Sample Answers
If twelve people observed the event, would they all come to the same conclusion?	It's hard to get a dozen people to agree on anything unless the proof of a proposition is ironclad. I don't have ironclad proof of my belief, so further clarity is in order.
What part of my thinking is likely to be rational and verifiable?	I don't like anyone snubbing me. That's a fact. However, I have no undisputed proof, now, of whether I'm right or wrong in my assumptions about Pat. That's a fact, too. Note: this phase of clarity is often easy to achieve because it's uncomplicated.

What part of my thinking is likely to be parasitic and disconfirmable?	When you get into parasitic thinking areas, you are likely to discover complications. You declare that Pat *is* a rotten person. The verb *to be* is the clue to this overgeneralization. The verb *is* says that you can only view Pat one way. We know that's not true. So, we have a conflict between language and reality. A major change comes with turning Pat's non-greeting into *action* instead of *being*. To do this, you shift from thinking that Pat *is* X (a global rating about Pat's identity) to rating Pat's actions. This leads you out of the trap where if you *are* only one way, how can you *be* any different? If you learn that Pat intentionally snubbed you, you can fairly say that from your perspective, Pat *acted* rotten. Here is another disputation question that flows from clarity on what parasitic anger thinking is and is not: Even if you are reading the situation correctly, in the course of your life, how important is this event compared to millions of others?
Does my anger belief(s) help me achieve reasonable and constructive goals?	If I feel worse, and have revengeful thoughts, this hardly sounds like a means to an end of achieving reasonable and constructive goals.

Effects. By doing a double take on your thinking, you might rightly conclude that you don't know the causes and reasons for Pat's behavior. You don't know if Pat acted intentionally or was figuratively asleep at the wheel when passing you. Your anger subsides. You have now created a favorable new effect for yourself.

When you do an ABCDE analysis, you don't assume that Pat did not snub you. The purpose is to isolate and rebut irrational, parasitic beliefs about the situation. Let's say Pat did intend to snub you. You might work on accepting what you don't like.

You can use other self-questioning methods. For example, here is a *scenario* question: What if Pat were deep in thought at the time? Here is a *role reversal* question: Should Pat feel angered by you because you passed by without saying "Hi"?

MY ABCDE EXPERIMENT

It's your turn to test the ABCDE method with an anger problem of your own using the following ABCDE chart. In the second column, first write down the activating event, or what happened. Second, write what you believe about the event. Third, describe how you felt (emotional consequences) and what you did (behavioral consequences). Fourth, dispute the belief(s) using the four basic questions we covered above. And fifth, describe the effects that occurred, if any, by following this process.

The ABCDEs of Positive Change	Responses
Activating Event	
Beliefs About the Event	
Emotional and Behavioral Consequences	
The Four Basic Dispute Questions 1. If twelve people observed the event, would they all come to the same conclusion? 2. What part of my thinking is likely to be rational and verifiable? 3. What part of my thinking is likely to be parasitic and disconfirmable? 4. Does my anger belief(s) help me achieve reasonable and constructive goals?	
Effects	

You can use this ABCDE exercise with practically all emotionally charged parasitic thinking situations that you choose to address, such as anxiety at the thought of rejection.

BREAK THE PARASITIC RULES

The last approach toward positive change that we'll cover in this chapter involves learning to replace parasitic rules with more rational beliefs based on probability. To do this, let's look at some other common irrational beliefs.

Irrational Beliefs

Albert Ellis identified three irrational beliefs that are at the heart of much needless human misery: a dire need for perfection, approval, and comfort. It's helpful to look at the three needs as parasitic rules with the power to trigger anger thinking, anger arousal, and anger actions. Here are how these parasitic thinking rules apply:

Rule 1. *I must* achieve perfection in every way, *or else* I am a failure and a horrible person.

Rule 2. *You must* love me and treat me as I wish, *or else* you are a horrible person who deserves severe punishment.

Rule 3. *Life must* be fair and easy. Otherwise, life sucks and is horrible.

Depending on the way you view violations of these rules, you may experience anger, self-doubts, anxiety, depression, or combinations of these unpleasant states. For example, if under rule 2 someone disrespects you, ignores you, doesn't show enough adoration, or doesn't include you in an activity (as you believe they should), then they deserve to be staked to the ground and covered with fire ants. In this scenario, you believe the other person must comply with what you demand. That's a tad self-centered, wouldn't you say?

There is no universal law or popular value system that requires you, or any other person on the planet, to unwaveringly adhere to the three rules as conditions that are absolute, necessary, and without exception.

The Probability Option

Part of your cognitive world revolves around categories, degrees, and probabilities. For example, oranges and grasshoppers are both living things but fall into different categories. The color orange exists in shades from light to dark. The probability is close to 100% that both oranges and grasshoppers will be part of our physical world next year and that colors will continue to have different shades.

The probability world is different from the black-and-white world where you are either a winner or a loser, good or bad, angry or kind. The box below shows a shift from irrational, categorical rules we saw in the previous section to a probability view.

Probability 1. If I make a good faith effort, I'll likely do well.

Probability 2. If I treat you well, there is a higher probability that you'll reciprocate in positive ways than if I treat you poorly.

Probability 3. If I put in the effort to learn and do things to improve my life, I'll get further faster than if I insist on a life of automatic ease and comfort.

To remind yourself to break parasitic rules, create a wallet-sized card with the above three probability statements, which you can download and print at http://www.newharbinger.com/44321. Apply it in situations where you might have previously angered yourself as a result of irrational rules. See if you create a different effect.

MY PROGRESS LOG

Key ideas: What three ideas did you pick up from this chapter that you found most helpful?

1.

2.

3.

Action plan: What three steps would you take to move closer to overcoming anger excesses?

1.

2.

3.

Execution: What are you going to do to execute the steps? (The process)

1.

2.

3.

Results: What do you hope to learn—or have reinforced—by taking these steps?

1.

2.

3.

Revisions: If you would make changes in the process, what would you do differently next time?

1.

2.

3.

CHAPTER 4

Your Perspective Solution

Imagine you are on the top of a mountain, standing on a tower. You look around you. You have a panoramic view of the trees that make up the forest. Below, you see a river winding through the land. You see a small town in the distance, and so much more. Now, imagine yourself standing still. You take a sheet of paper and roll it into a narrow tube, where one end is wide enough to go over an eye, and the other end narrows to a tiny opening. Now, close your left eye and look through the tube with your right. The town is there. The river is there. The trees that make up the forest are there.

You no longer have your normal panoramic view. Instead, you've closed an eye and looked at the world around you through a narrow tube. The lesson of this exercise is that it's what you don't see that is often important.

Anger narrows perspective. The tunnel vision of anger is functional in physical threat situations. It's part of nature's survival plan. You'll impede your survival if you watch a bird in flight when you're under attack. Parasitic anger presents a different picture. The danger is to your image, beliefs, personal rules, expectations, and more (ego threats). Absorb yourself in this narrow world, and not much else matters except satisfying the voracious appetite of this parasitic ego.

When parasitic anger narrows your psychological perspective, you'll have trouble seeing from another's vantage point. This loss of perspective amplifies anger (Yip and Schweitzer 2019).

If you find yourself in this perspective-narrowing trap, how do you ditch the tube? Deliberately look from different angles at what's going on. Put CBT tools to work, such as cognitive reappraisal, ABCDE methods, and distancing techniques, to help expand your perspective.

In this chapter, we'll cover the following ways to broaden your perspective and see both the forest and the trees:

- learn to recognize and break free from circular reasoning and overgeneralization traps,

- experiment with questions of inquiry and strategy to shift from parasitic anger to a reality-based perspective,

- free yourself from parasitic anger by projecting short-term and long-term results,

- use humorous exaggerations to change your mood and distance yourself from parasitic anger thinking, and

- understand the positive-perspective triad and how it can help reduce anger and its harmful effects in your life.

TWO CLASSIC CONSTRICTIONS ON PERSPECTIVE

Anger problems and bitter feelings amplify each other; when you are intolerant of both, your perspective narrows. Circular reasoning and overgeneralization are perspective-narrowing experiences that help propel this narrowing. Let's look at how you can free yourself from these constraints.

Circular Reasoning

Circular reasoning is a logical fallacy where you figuratively go around in circles, starting with one idea and then ending with a conclusion that is the same as or similar to the original idea. For example:

- "I'm mad because you made me mad."

- "I must have my way so that I won't get angry, and I won't get angry when I get my way."

Some circular reasoning involves three nodes on the circle: primary premise, secondary premise, and conclusion:

- Your *primary premise* is "I'm entitled to get my way."

- Your *secondary premise* (why anger is a necessary response to any frustration where you see yourself as thwarted) is "It is an absolute disaster if I don't."

- Your *conclusion* is "I must get my way."

Punch holes in any part of this process, and you can exit the circle.

Here is how to use *because interventions* to punch holes in the process:

- Your primary premise: "I'm entitled to get my way."

  - You ask yourself, *Because?*

  - You respond, *Because it's my birthright, because I believe I am special, and because I believe that I am deserving.* What is the validity of any of that?

- Your secondary premise: "It is an absolute disaster if I don't."

  - You ask yourself, *Because?*

  - You respond, *Because I can't stand feeling frustrated, because there is a universal law that all must accommodate me, and because the world will come to an end if I don't get my way.* (Your *because* answer also circles back to the primary premise.) What is the validity of that?

■ Your conclusion: "I must get my way."

• You ask yourself, *Because?*

• You respond, *Because it is my birthright, because I can't stand not having what I want, and because I'll get angry if I don't get my way.* (Again, your *because* answer circles back to the primary premise.) What is the validity of any of that?

Circular reasoning could have an unstated conclusion that is the same as the premise "My life would be great if other people didn't mess with me (and because they mess with me, my life isn't great)." When this circle eludes your detection, you have an anger blind spot. That blind spot will probably extend to blame and to justify aggression. Catch yourself spinning in this circle, and this awareness may be enough for you to break free from the loop.

Overgeneralizing

Women *are* bad drivers. Men *are* slobs. What do these examples have in common? In single phrases, I pigeonholed both genders, thus demonstrating two overgeneralizations. Here's how it works with parasitic anger. You shout at your mate, "You *are* a worthless idiot!" How do you get out of this overgeneralization trap?

Is it just the words "bad," "slobs," and "idiot" that, in the right context, can arouse anger? Let's probe a bit deeper and see if there is a common connection. Does the verb "to be" influence an outpouring of angry feelings? After all, if a person *is* one way at this moment, one is likely to form a perspective of the individual as being that way in general.

Alfred Korzybski (1933), the founder of a therapy approach called general semantics, saw a danger in what he termed the "*is* of identity." The single verb obliterated the complexity of a human being. In this context, he saw the verb "is" as representing a primitive, restrictive, fallacious, unjustified evaluation. The more abstract the *is of identity* phrase (bad, good, pleasant, unpleasant), the higher the risk for misreading situations and for the excess tension that comes in the form of an unjustified "is of identity" evaluation.

Character overgeneralizations, like bad drivers, slobs, and worthless idiots, are examples of extension-of-blame thinking. These overgeneralizations are irrational and challengeable on numerous grounds. They are like a weak opponent puffed up to look all-powerful. To sap these parasites of their power, look for exceptions to the overgeneralizations. Normally you won't have far to look.

NASCAR race car drivers Danica Patrick and Tammy Jo Kirk dispel the myth that all women are bad drivers. And true, some men trash their living quarters, but the majority do not. How about those who are compulsively clean? If your mate is a worthless idiot, what does that say about your choice? Might you see your mate differently at a different time?

The general semanticists D. David Bourland and Paul Johnston (1991) suggested using active verbs to describe actions, thereby eliminating the verb "to be." They called this E-prime, or English language minus the verb "to be." Let's see how you might do this. "I don't like how some women drive." "I'd prefer that men disavowed sloppiness." By defining what you don't like or would prefer, you shift needless blame away from others. At the same time, you assert your right to dislike what you dislike. Additionally, you distance yourself from character overgeneralizations and extension-of-blame thinking.

Communications with the verb "to be" work fine most of the time. However, when the *is of identity* helps drive parasitic anger patterns, intentionally eliminating the verb, in special circumstances, can promote a more objective perspective. The following exercise will help you put this into practice.

MY OVERGENERALIZING EXPERIMENT

Blame-labeling people with *is of identity* labels can evoke and justify angry feelings on your part as well as theirs. Instead, you might use E-prime for stripping away a parasitic factor from your anger. The following shows contrasting approaches.

Parasitic Anger Thinking	E-Prime Thinking
Jake *is* a complete idiot.	When Jake insults his boss, he *acts* foolishly.

Most people are so well practiced in *is of identity* thinking that it comes naturally. But by substituting the word "act" for "is," this creates a different perspective in which the focus is on Jake's behavior rather than on his identity.

Making yourself aware of this *is of identity* process is challenging, but you can slow the process. One way is to judge *acts*. The following chart contrasts an *act* perspective with an *is of identity* perspective.

Situation	*Is of Identity* Perspective	*Act* Perspective
You are looking forward to a quiet dinner at your favorite restaurant when a group of people sit at the table beside you and laugh and speak loudly in celebration of someone's birthday.	These people *are* a bunch of illiterate loudmouths who *should be* drinking sulfuric acid soup. That would shut them up.	I don't like the way this group *acts*.
	Accuracy of *Is of Identity* Perspective	**Accuracy of *Act* Perspective**
	I have no evidence that everyone in the group always acts and thinks the same way. I muddle clarity and trouble myself when I categorize and extend blame for something I don't like. They came to the restaurant for a different purpose than I did.	I don't like loud conversations. They occupy themselves with their agenda and are seemingly mindless of their surroundings. I'd prefer that they dial down the volume.

It's your turn to strengthen your reasoning skills by moving from overgeneralizing *is of identity thinking* to that of evaluating acts. Pick a recent situation in which *is of identity* was an anger factor. Which perspective can you more easily verify?

Situation	*Is of Identity* Perspective	*Act* Perspective
	Accuracy of *Is of Identity* Perspective	**Accuracy of *Act* Perspective**

When viewing people in terms of their acts rather than their global being, you are likely to promote clarity in support of a reasoned perspective. Your perspective and options broaden. You avoid your anger becoming the issue. That is a victory.

TWO QUESTIONING TECHNIQUES

A well-worded question contains the conditions for its answer. Let's look at questions of inquiry and strategy. *Questions of inquiry* are the analytic phase of a two-part problem-solving process. *Questions of strategy* are about what to do.

Questions of Inquiry

Inquiry questions are open-ended and can include *what, when, where, why,* and *how* probes. They can be particularly useful for probing parasitic anger beliefs and the fallacies in these beliefs. Two sample questions of inquiry and sample answers follow:

- Question: What would happen if any time someone acted in a way I didn't like, I held the view that the person deserved to be fire-bombed by a drone? Sample answer: If everyone, at various times, acted displeasingly and thereby deserved this punishment, no one would go unpunished.

- Question: If I feel tense, uncomfortable, and angry for no visible reason, what's my purpose for blaming someone? Sample answer: Misplaced blame serves the purpose of attributing a cause, thus stirring up animosity, whereas acceptance of unexplained reasons is the enlightened approach.

Strategy Questions

For our purposes, strategy questions piggyback on answers to inquiry questions. Strategy questions are for eliciting reasonable action approaches to overcome a problem. Two sample questions of strategy and sample answers follow:

- Question: When I don't like what someone says, does, or doesn't do, what are my rational options? Sample answer: (1) I can start by accepting the situation. (2) I can communicate what I don't like without being aggressive (see chapter 10). (3) I'll focus on the problem and steer clear from personality issues. (4) I'll avoid the accusatory *you*, which sounds like I'm blaming and complaining. (5) If I hit a wall, I'll try a different way or unblinkingly accept that you can't get through to everyone. (6) If I discover an error in my actions, I'll accept responsibility for that. (7) If I need to take further steps, I'll take them.

- Question: How do I gain clarity when, seemingly from out of the blue, I feel tense, uncomfortable, and angry? Sample answer: (1) I'll accept that tension and discomfort are signals, and there may be no visible answer as to the causes. (2) I'll look for patterns: When has this happened before? Was there an observable cause? (3) When the cause of the signal is unclear, rather than jumping to conclusions and arbitrarily blaming someone, I'll suspend judgment until I have clarity or it's clear that my temporary mood and irritable state was the cause.

MY INQUIRY AND STRATEGY QUESTIONING EXPERIMENT

You can build questions of inquiry and strategy into an approach similar to the ABCDE process, but with different categories. Here's how:

Event	1. I can't locate a container of fast-dry glue at a large warehouse store.
	2. I can't find an employee available to help.
Belief	1. Management is stupid for not having enough staff available.
	2. The staff are lazy and don't do their job. Management should fire them, and would if management were competent.
Inquiry Questions	1. Where is it written that store employees must be available at my beck and call?
	2. If I find no one available, where is the proof that all store employees are lazy?
Strategy Questions	1. What would I do if the store were completely self-service?
	2. Can I find a checkout clerk to point me toward the product?
	3. Where is the manager located so I can ask?
Outcome	Inquiry Questions:
	1. It's preferable if an employee is available to help, but not the end of the world if none is.
	2. I've made a correctable fundamental attribution error. There is no proof that all employees are lazy. There is, however, proof that none are currently available.
	Strategy Answers:
	1. I'd look in areas where I might find glue, such as crafts. No luck.
	2. There are long lines at each checkout counter. No luck.
	3. In looking for a manager, I found a service area. I asked about the glue and was directed to an aisle.

Now it's your turn to give this a try to see if the approach works for you.

Event	
Belief	
Inquiry Questions	
Strategy Questions	
Outcome	Inquiry Questions: Strategy Answers:

PROJECTING SHORT-TERM AND LONG-TERM RESULTS

A short- and long-term assessment of a parasitic anger situation is a quick and simple thing to do that can be surprisingly effective. You look at the short- and long-term advantages of parasitic anger thinking and the short- and long-term advantages of challenging parasitic thinking. Then, make your choice! Here is an example:

Perspective	Advantages of Parasitic Anger Thinking	Advantages of Challenging Parasitic Thinking
Short-Term	Can get immediate relief from venting or striking out impulsively.	Learning and practicing new ways to broaden and maintain a realistic perspective using enlightened choices. Avoiding acting impulsively and possibly destructively. Widening perspective and putting realistic priorities about the matter into motion.
Long-Term	There are no meaningful long-term advantages other than short-term specious rewards that repeat themselves.	Superior sense of command over myself when facing undesirable conditions. Growing ability to restrict and restrain parasitic thinking. Greater freedom to constructively express natural anger toward unfair situations and to do so proportionately. Increased probability of avoiding prolonged periods of thinking negatively (ruminating), catastrophizing, and other unwanted effects, such as hammering away at my body with stress hormone surges.

It's your turn to try this method to help switch course from a parasitic to a parasite-constraining approach.

MY SHORT- AND LONG-TERM PARASITIC ANGER THINKING ASSESSMENT

Think about what you have learned about parasitic anger thinking and ways to challenge that thinking. Fill in the table below with advantages of both types of thinking from your perspective.

Perspective	Advantages of Parasitic Anger Thinking	Advantages of Challenging Parasitic Thinking
Short-Term		
Long-Term		

A longer-term perspective can short-circuit impulsive acts for short-term relief and help you widen your perspective to avoid parasitic anger recurrences.

HUMOROUS EXAGGERATIONS: WHAT'S A BLAME BELIEF WORTH?

It's rarely a good idea to ridicule yourself for parasitic anger thinking. However, you might benefit from poking fun at the parasitic beliefs and ideals themselves.

Let's suppose you tried to sell your parasitic anger beliefs. Here is a possible advertisement: "Thirty ways to add excitement to your life by demanding the impossible and following up with blame fests when you don't achieve it. Experience the stimulation of angering yourself as often as you wish." Do you think the idea would have broad appeal and sell? Does this humorous exaggeration put the worth of parasitic thinking into a different perspective?

MY HUMOROUS EXAGGERATION EXPERIMENT

Humorous exaggerations can put parasitic anger demands and their extensions into a humorous perspective. Here is an example.

Blame Belief	Sales Pitch	Expected Result
You should always get what you expect, and those who stand in your way will have plenty to regret.	A demanding life is a place to be. There is no need to set yourself free. Parasitic anger is the key.	Selling parasitic anger views is a tough sell, especially since so many people create their demons and don't need extra help.

It's your turn to try your humorous sales pitch. Write down one of your blame beliefs, and then come up with a sales pitch and expected result of the sales pitch.

Blame Belief	Sales Pitch	Expected Result

When you are laughing and having a good time putting parasitic ideas on the run, you can't be simultaneously experiencing parasitic anger.

THE POSITIVE-PERSPECTIVE TRIAD

Below we'll look at a positive perspective triad composed of objective self-observation, confident composure, and realistic optimism to replace parasitic anger perspectives.

Objective Self-Observation

When you observe provocative experiences through objective lenses and turn those lenses inwardly on your thoughts and feelings, you are likely to get a sharper focus on that elusive state called reality. If you know the triggers, signs, and causes of anger, self-observation can replace a parasitic anger reaction with a reflective response. Accurate explanations can help you quell needless anger, reduce the problem to its essentials, and develop reasonable perspectives based on facts, reason, and knowledge that can extend into effective actions.

Confident Composure

Confident composure is a state of mind where you feel in charge of yourself and the controllable events around you. With confident composure, you recognize that you can directly command only yourself, and you choose to do so. You don't demand that the world change for you, as this is unrealistic. You take life and situations as they are. You drive your actions with productive intentions. You allow yourself to live with the natural tensions that signal problems to solve and that are a normal part of this form of exploration. With this flexible and stronger view, your psychological resources are more available to advance your enlightened self-interests.

You can gain confident composure skills by addressing needless anger and selectively facing adversities that are harmful when avoided. By recognizing and defusing misguiding anger thinking, you are less likely to waste your time with these distractions.

Realistic Optimism

Believe that you can apply your talents and learn new ways to combat parasitic anger now, and you are thinking like a realistic optimist. As a realistic optimist, you don't wait for things to happen. You create opportunities to increase positive experiences and reduce negative ones (which is also positive).

You believe you can reduce parasitic anger because you are confident that you can build the necessary skills. You ground that belief in objective self-observations. You believe that by persisting, you'll continue improving, and so you persist. That's realistic optimism!

As a realistic optimist, you'll be more inclined than most to cope proactively. Proactive coping is where you anticipate an upcoming stressor. You seize on the opportunity to prepare yourself for the event, possibly averting it (Aspinwall 2011). Aspiring for a positive future and setting the stage to successfully achieve positive future goals is associated with emotional well-being (Sohl and Moyer 2009).

Proactive coping is about reducing negatives and increasing positives. This is a useful tool for the realistic optimist's toolbox.

MY PROGRESS LOG

Key ideas: What three ideas did you pick up from this chapter that you found most helpful?

1.

2.

3.

Action plan: What three steps would you take to move closer to overcoming anger excesses?

1.

2.

3.

Execution: What are you going to do to execute the steps? (The process)

1.

2.

3.

Results: What do you hope to learn—or have reinforced—by taking these steps?

1.

2.

3.

Revisions: If you would make changes in the process, what would you do differently next time?

1.

2.

3.

CHAPTER 5

Coping with Unfairness

Unfairness is provocative, and anger is a common response. Yet this is often an understated issue in many books on anger. Nevertheless, since the dawning of humanity, anger toward unfairness has been a natural response. Parasitic anger toward real or imagined unfairness, however, is like a self-inflicted wound that can hurt a lot.

Let's take an excursion into the world of unfairness and explore resolutions. Together, we'll look at

- aspects of unfairness, including aversion for unfairness, what makes a system unfair, and types of fairness systems;

- the importance of judging accurately who is trustworthy and who is not, and why the way you handle yourself in such circumstances makes a big difference;

- the importance of taking a "trust but verify" approach;

- ways to combat the "parasitic enemy within" (parasitic anger) through preference language;

- the 7-R action plan for mapping alternative ways to respond to harmful, unfair actions and practices; and

- the connection between reactance (a perception of unfairly losing privileges), anger, and fairness.

THE UNFAIRNESS PUZZLE

What is this thing called unfairness? *Unfairness refers to inequitable, unjust, or unreasonable behavior on the part of one person or group against another. These acts result in harm and losses to another.* Understandably, people treated unfairly don't like it.

If you ask people for examples of what raises their anger temperature, you'll hear plenty of stories—often related to unfairness. Here are some common ones: A coworker takes credit for your work and gets the promotion you wanted. A car dealer sells you a lemon without telling you it was in floodwaters. Your homeowner's association board abuses its authority and makes life hard for you. When it comes to seriously unfair situations, calmly taking it on the chin rarely works out well. Measured and directed anger (free of parasitic elements, of course) is appropriate.

You don't have to be perfect (i.e., never acted unfairly yourself) to address unfairness. You have a right to combat unfair practices, especially events that impede your enlightened interests (see chapters 9 and 10 on assertiveness methods). At the same time, keep the following phrases in mind: "choose your battles wisely" (i.e., address priorities that are worth fighting for) and "some things are not worth the fight" (i.e., make responsible choices as to how you'll use your time and resources).

To better understand the role of unfairness in anger, below we'll explore aversion for unfairness, unfair systems, and fairness systems.

Aversion for Unfairness

An aversion for unfairness has biological roots and can surface as early as twelve to eighteen months of age (Geraci and Surian 2011; Sloane, Baillargeon, and Premack 2012; Wang and Henderson 2018). Even if you are a third-party observer of an unfair action against another, you might experience empathetic anger in support of the unfairly treated person (Landmann and Hess 2017).

If you could hop in a time machine and go back 200,000 years or more, you'd likely see a primal reaction to unfairness. Your ancient ancestors survived and thrived through trust and cooperative efforts. Unfair actions threatened that cooperative effort. If someone took an unearned share of food another worked hard to obtain, this would likely activate the unfairness circuit in the brain, propelling anger to correct the inequity.

You can find examples of unfair practices in practically every recorded era. For example, seventeenth-century English scholar Edward Reynolds described unfair practices when he wrote that people provoke anger in others through manipulations, falsehoods, and pretenses of plausibility (consolidated from different sections from Reynolds, 1656).

We're not the only ones with an aversion to inequity. In the famous *Animal Planet* "Meerkat Manor" TV series, outliers caught stealing lost face in the community (Bekoff and Pierce 2009). When a pet dog sees another dog get a bigger reward for doing the same thing, the cheated dog goes on strike (McGetrick and Range 2018; Range et al. 2009). Brown capuchin monkeys in captivity respond negatively to inequitable rewards and throw the lesser reward at the person who shortchanged them (Brosnan and de Waal 2003). Wild Taï chimpanzees distribute meat based on the hunters' skills (Boesch 2002). In humans, too, inequity is gut-wrenching enough that most people will take a personal loss rather than accept an unfair deal (Gabay et al. 2014).

Unfair Systems

In our human societies, unfairness is typically a three-phase process involving *motives*, *deceptive processes*, and *unmerited outcomes*. Here is a widely publicized example: In March 2019, a college admission scandal made the news. Over fifty people allegedly paid between $15,000 and over $1 million to educational consultant William "Rick" Singer to get their kids into prestigious colleges. As it was reported, in some cases, Singer had confederates take college-entry tests for his clients' kids. In other cases, he made his clients' nonathletic kids look like sports stars and bribed school athletic coaches to champion the students' applications.

Here is how the parents' behavior matches the three-phase process. The parents

1. acted out of selfishness to benefit their kids (the motive),

2. hired Singer to cheat for them (the deceptive process), and

3. advantaged their kids by bumping better-qualified students (the unmerited outcome).

These unfair acts evoked public outrage.

The following chart describes forms of anger-evoking unfairness and examples of each. You'll find assertive ways to respond in chapters 9 and 10.

Unfair Processes	Examples
Adverse Inequity	Brushing aside community norms, rules, and standards and taking more than what's merited.
Favoritism	Dispensing or receiving an undeserved advantage because of nepotism, political connections, and other inequities.
Deception	Concealing motivations to fool others to gain advantages or benefits through omitting or mispresenting information.
Cheating	Making false statements on employment applications, getting examination answers through an earpiece, claiming someone's work as your own.
Exploitation	Manipulation, misrepresentation, conniving, or scamming to gain an unfair advantage, leaving the other worse off.
Coverup	Deflecting blame and avoiding responsibility to maintain a positive public image; blaming the exploited person for what you are doing.

Finding the Invisible Elephant

The famous Russian fabulist, Ivan Krilof (Ralston 1869, 43), introduced the concept of the invisible elephant in the room in his tale of *The Inquisitive Man*. While visiting a museum, a man attended to so many small details that he missed the elephant in the room. His friend asked, "But did you see the elephant?" The man responded, "Are you quite sure it's there?"

In the world of deception, language is the invisible elephant. Thus, a sincere-sounding smooth talker can distract others from seeing unfair practices. The emergence of language may have opened more new ways for deception than for honest communication (Dor 2017).

How do you use the concept of the invisible elephant? Focus on the big picture, on what is relevant, and on what is the responsible thing to do. That's the quickest path through deceptive verbiage.

How do you recognize an abusive fiction? Philosopher of science Karl Popper (1992) wrote that if you can't test and falsify (show to be untrue) a statement, it pays to be skeptical of it. For example, if you believe that angels dance on the heads of pins, how can you subject this belief to a test to see if you can falsify it? You can't. Therefore, the statement is fiction until you can.

How do you respond to unfairness? The ancient Greek Philosopher Aristotle shared this view:

Both fear and confidence and appetite and anger and pity and in general pleasure and pain may be felt both too much and too little, and in both cases not well; but to feel them at the right times, with reference to the right objects, towards the right people, with the right motive, and in the right way, is what is both intermediate and best, and this is characteristic of virtue. (Aristotle 1999, 27)

So how do we see the elephant in the room? By exploring fairness systems, you'll get an expanded picture of the elephant by seeing what others have found relevant. I'll turn to that next.

Fairness Systems

Social fairness systems have existed since the start of civilization and have evolved with population growth. The following chart describes common fairness systems for guiding behavior and lowering the risk of exploitation, which is a threat to fairness, trust, and cooperation.

Fairness Systems	Description and Examples
Procedural Fairness (Justice)	Standard policies, practices, and processes for resolving disputes that are equal for all.
Distributive Fairness (Justice)	Distributing opportunities, goods, and ownership according to merit and for the best interests of society.
Equality Fairness	A level playing field for goods and opportunities. Supermarket prices are the same for all. You are free to run a race as fast as you can.

Rule-Based Fairness	Following the rules when playing a game.
Practical Fairness	Advantaging your family and friends without needlessly harming others; not revealing your strategy when competing against a rival.
Self-Interest Fairness	Implementing rules you believe to be fair. For example, parents ground a teen for staying out too late. The parents view it as warranted, corrective, and fair, while the teen thinks the punishment is excessive and unfair. Both may be right. What you think is fair will sometimes clash with other views that are valid.

Some fairness rules and procedures are more elastic than others. You show up fifteen minutes late for a lunch meeting one day. You might get a comment. Do this routinely, and you stretch the limits too far; that's unfair to others who wait.

TRUST VERSUS DISTRUST

What is this thing called trust? *When you act in a trustworthy manner, you act equitably, open-mindedly, and reasonably. You reciprocate. Your dealings with others tend to be just but not necessarily equal.*

Your amygdala, which you met in chapter 2, senses whether you can trust or distrust someone. Although others can sometimes fool the amygdala, it's like a sixth sense, or intuitive ability, that exists beyond your conscious awareness. If you have an initial impression of distrust for someone, it will be difficult to change that impression if you are wrong. The amygdala is slow to change.

How are trust and fairness related? People whom you have cause to trust are likely those who act fairly toward you. Trust binds people together, makes cooperation feasible, and plays a pivotal role in almost every aspect of human life and relationships (Lu et al. 2019).

Whom Do You Trust?

Among the people you know well, you probably have a good idea of whom to trust. To a significant degree, people you trust are likely to

- stick with you under adverse conditions,

- watch out for your interests,

- act with integrity toward you,

- work to maintain an agreeable relationship,

- show trustworthy judgments,

- live up to agreements, and

- act with reasonable competence.

When these seven factors are reciprocal, you have a trustworthy relationship.

Whom Do You Distrust?

Significant norm violations promote distrust (Haesevoets et al. 2018). Distrust promotes social instability, and this is a hair trigger for anger and aggressive responses (Eriksson, Andersson, and Strimling 2017).

Your ability to detect unfairness and untrustworthiness is so important that a significant part of your brain is involved in appraising the trustworthiness of strangers, picking up on changes in a person's tone, and assessing the truth in what people say. Among the people you know, you probably have a good idea of whom to distrust because they

- acted in one or more unfair ways toward you,

- caused you to watch your back on one or more occasions,

- intentionally concealed matters of material importance from you,

- lied to you in ways that caused you harm,

- took advantage of you,

- acted duplicitously,

- reneged on agreements or commitments, or

- performed incompetently when, with a little extra effort, they could have gotten it right.

These eight unfairness factors are prime sources of distrust.

TRUST BUT VERIFY

It's better to trust and cooperate than to mistrust and oppose others, as this is both functional and less stressful. Trustworthy people are likely to earn higher incomes and lead healthier and happier lives compared to those whose minds overflow with hostile, cynical beliefs (Stavrova and Ehlebracht 2016). However, trust need not be blind. With unfamiliar people, or with people with questionable motives, it is important to think things through, separate fact from fiction, and not rely too much on gut impressions (Ma-Kellams and Lerner 2016).

The fortieth US president, Ronald Reagan, understood this reality principle well. In his January 11, 1989, *Farewell to the Nation* address, Ronald Reagan offered this advice on trust and distrust: "At first, pull your punches. If they persist, pull the plug. It's still trust but verify. It's still play but cut the cards. It's still watch closely. And don't be afraid to see what you see" (the Public Papers of President Ronald W. Reagan, Ronald Reagan Presidential Library, https://www.reaganlibrary.gov/research/speeches/011189i).

The benefits of having a trusting attitude is that of personability and better relationships with people. The benefit of verifying facts is showing you are not a pushover. That's a powerful combination.

COMBATTING THE PARASITIC ENEMY WITHIN THROUGH LANGUAGE

Every society has rules, codes, and traditions. Most people have their personal golden books of standards as well. Some might take the form of demands, such as, "You must not inconvenience me. I must have what I need. You must comply or else." This demandingness is a cognitive component of anger (Buschmann et al. 2018; Vîslă et al. 2016).

Albert Ellis saw anger in irrational demands for fairness: "Things like justice, fairness, equity, and democracy must prevail" (Ellis 1977, 43). Here are three extension-of-blame examples:

- It's unfair for anybody to deceive you. Therefore, the person(s) must not do that. Violators deserve severe punishment.

- It's unfair for anybody to take advantage of you. Therefore, the person(s) should not do that. Violators deserve severe punishment.

- It's unfair for anybody to fool you into doing something that causes you a loss. Therefore, the person(s) ought not to do that. Violators deserve severe punishment.

The first sentence in each of the three examples is reasonable. The second can evoke parasitic anger. The third justifies reprisals based on a parasitic perspective. Neo-analyst Karen Horney described this demandingness as "the tyranny of the should." The demander thinks these insistences are reasonable. Yet the reaction is out of proportion to the provocative situations (Horney 1950).

If you stir yourself up with demandingness, you can calm your thinking and still respond proportionally by asking yourself three questions.

Three Questions for Clarity

If you inflame yourself with demandingness thinking, you risk muddling your mind as you stress your body. You'll probably lose perspective. The following three questions, and sample answers, can broaden options that are in concert with your enlightened interests.

Questions for Clarity	Sample Answers
Does demanding fairness support the achievement of my constructive interests and goals?	A demand for fairness is a common prelude to extension-of-blame thinking and clouding your thoughts with the fog of anger. This mindset will usually distract you from your positive goals.
Does demanding fairness help foster healthy relationships with others?	Anger expressed through extension-of-blame thinking can decrease your chances for support from others. You may come across as unpleasant.
Does demanding fairness lead to a proportional response?	Demandingness narrows your focus to an expectation, which, if thwarted, can lead to an anger excess.

If you find yourself in the demandingness trap, can you exit?

Using Preference Language to Lessen Anger

A tripwire for parasitic anger is demanding, expecting, requiring, and insisting that you must, ought to, and should have things go your way and should be treated fairly. Given this entitlement view, you are likely to experience a boomerang effect with some others who don't share your positions.

Preference thinking is about what most people want or desire, such as fair and equitable treatment, freedom from deceptions, reciprocity, trust, and cooperation. The words are different from the language of *should*, *ought*, and *must*. Preference thinking is about what you *want*, *like*, and *prefer*.

Each language style represents a different philosophy. Demand and preference philosophies can trigger different feelings about the same situation. The following chart shows the contrast:

Demanding Philosophy	Preferring Philosophy
Expect	Prefer
Require	Want
Must	Desire
Need	Like
Should	Allow
Insist	Consider
Ought	Rather

Can you feel a difference between requiring and preferring words?

Putting Preference Thinking into Action

In chapter 2, you found three dimensions of unconditional acceptance—accepting yourself, others, and life. You learned that acceptance defuses parasitic anger without diminishing your right to hold others accountable. Now, let's explore how demanding and preference thinking influence how you feel and what you do.

You planned to meet some work acquaintances at a restaurant. You showed. They didn't. Your first thoughts were that they went somewhere else without telling you, which they *should not* have done to you. You extend the blame by thinking something like *They (the acquaintances) are unfair, inconsiderate, rotten scoundrels who deserve to be stung by woolly recluse spiders.*

Preference thinking keeps it simple. You might avoid jumping to conclusions and avoid extension-of-blame thinking and vengeful impulses. The following chart provides a contrast between a demanding view and a preference view.

Demanding View	Preference View
People *must* treat me fairly, or they are horrible and deserve punishment.	I *prefer* fair treatment. I don't like it when someone mistreats me. Still, the world doesn't end when this happens.
My friends made new plans that excluded me; that's unfair, and they *must not* do that.	It would have been *desirable* for my friends to include me in the new plan. However, that is not a reason that they *must* do so.
People who unfairly try to exploit me deserve to suffer forever.	I wish only fair-minded people populated the world. That's not to be. I'll address such problems as I'm aware of them.

With a demanding philosophy in play, you externalize responsibility. You are likely to anger yourself parasitically and stew in your emotional juices. The pain you think others deserve you bring upon yourself. Is that being fair to yourself? Probably not! You run the risk of embitterment where you are likely to be prone to finding and lamenting injustices and unfairnesses. Proneness to embitterment can warp your values, impede your flexibility to adjust, and affect your health. Reminding yourself to keep an open mind to experiences and seek positive new experiences helps counter embitterment (Muschalla and von Kenne 2020).

Preferential thinking is compatible with an acceptance philosophy that is contrary to embitterment thinking. You may dislike unjust and unfair actions by others; however, you don't exaggerate the meaning of events and go on a vendetta as you might if guided by demandingness thinking and anger-related emotions.

Thinking preferentially, you can assert force in rectifying a wrong, with possibly higher effectiveness. That is because you allow yourself flexibility.

MY CONTRAST EXPERIMENT

The next time you are in an anger-triggering situation and are frothing with demandingness anger, remember what you are telling yourself. After that, create a contrast chart between demanding and preference thinking about the event. Which thinking is easier on your constitution?

CONTRAST CHART	
Demanding View	**Preference View**

Make copies of the chart, which you can download at http://www.newharbinger.com/44321. Try this experiment several times.

If you tend to be a visual thinker, the following *trouble* and *terrific* triangles can be a memorable way to compare the results of a demanding and a preferential view.

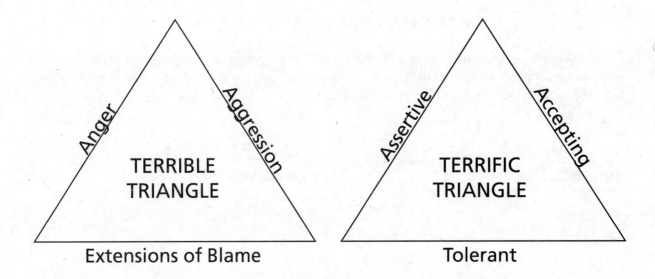

With practice in contrasting demanding and preference views, you can prime yourself to move in a more positive direction toward incorporating preference thinking at the time of an incident and avoid escalating anger. By learning and applying assertiveness techniques from chapters 9 and 10, I suspect you will build more confidence in the *terrific triangle* view.

THE 7-R ACTION PLAN

A chapter on the unfairness-anger connection would be incomplete without looking at behavioral responses to unfairness. Many of these responses are clustered around seven *R*s: *response cost, revenge, retaliation,* and *retribution* on the one hand; and *resolve, rectify, and remedy* on the other. I'll discuss these shortly.

Unfairness evolved over the millennia, and the level of complexities and complications of today would have boggled the minds of the first humans. Nowadays, if someone harms you by intentionally acting unfairly, you have a second unfairness to address, which is to rectify the wrong the other person caused. Without the original unfairness, you would not have to expend time and energy to resolve a problem that was not of your making. That's the way it goes sometimes.

Is it unfair that it takes an extra effort to rectify an intentionally created wrong? You bet it is. You don't have to like it. Accept that and you'll avoid distressing yourself about being in a position that warrants a response.

In the box below, write down an unfairness you are thinking about contesting. Keep this situation in mind as we explore the 7-R action plan next.

Finding the Right "R"

The following 7-R Action Plan chart lists the 7-R action factors, or response options, for unfair actions. You can use this chart (also available at http://www.newharbinger.com/44321) to help choose your action option—including that of taking no current action—to respond to the specific unfairness you wrote in the box above.

7-R ACTION PLAN

R-Responses
Response Cost: Imposing a cost on another to prevent the reoccurrence of harmful behavior. The idea is to stop the behavior. The response cost is enough to deter the behavior but no more.
Revenge: A bitter act against a person or group in response to prior harm. Revenge, executed in disregard to the law or social norms, such as keying another's car or throwing a brick through a window, is "wild justice."
Retaliation: Going *against* a prior negative action. In war, you counterattack with something of equal or greater intensity. On a personal level, you engage in payback for something said or done that was harmful to you.
Retribution: Legally prescribed punishment proportional to an offense to ensure justice for the victim and society. That is the role of the courts.
Resolve: Breaking down a problem into its components, deciding on a course of action(s), and preventing future episodes.
Rectify: Acting to set something right, restore a balance, or return a situation to its original status. You act to correct an inequity to your reasonable satisfaction.
Remedy: Seeking compensation for an injury sustained.

The famous blood feud between the Hatfields and McCoys shows a bitter cycle of hate-driven wild justice (Jones, 1948). Where's the satisfaction? If you try to reduce tension through revenge, you are likely to feel worse (Carlsmith, Wilson, and Gilbert 2008). And if you choose retribution, keep in mind that, in some situations, retribution is bittersweet (Eadeh, Peak, and Lambert 2017). Some things are resolvable between parties. Some are best left to the courts.

Questions to Consider Before Responding

Here are two questions to help you decide what actions—if any—you could take in your unfairness situation. The first question is about what you want to accomplish. The second is about the route you will take.

In the following chart, pencil in your goals and route (i.e., process) with regard to responding to the unfairness situation you wrote down earlier.

What do you want to accomplish that is constructive? (Consider whether you can do this.)
What route will you take? (Consider whether you are sticking within the norms and standards of your community or whether you are going out of bounds. If it's the latter, consider the risks in doing that.)

Your 7-R Decision

Now that you have learned the 7-R responses and explored the questions above, you are ready to put your skills into action. Next time you are in a situation requiring an *R* response, ask yourself, *What do I want to accomplish that is constructive? What route will I take?* If you choose to act, which of the 7-R responses is the most sensible? Write it in the following chart, along with your reason for choosing that response and how you will implement it.

Preferred R-Action	Reason for the Decision	Method of Implementation

Do you hold grudges and torment yourself over injustices, perhaps collecting them in your mind? While deciding your options about such matters, consider the importance of skills you learned in chapter 2: (1) ridding yourself of extension-of-blame thinking and (2) accepting what happened because it happened. You may still feel distrust. You may still want little to do with people who wronged you. However, you are less likely to figuratively eat away at yourself and more likely to have more energy to pursue positive things that matter.

THE REACTANCE-ANGER-FAIRNESS CONNECTION

Reactance is an unpleasant cognitive and emotive feeling about losing freedoms and privileges where you feel motivated to combat the threat or restore the right (Brehm and Brehm 1981). When you experience anger from the risk or a loss of a privilege or freedom, that's *reactance anger*.

People of all ages experience reactance. A teen deprived of the use of the family car says it's unfair and experiences reactance anger when the loss seems excessive. When pressured to think or act a certain way, you might experience reactance anger. For example, an elected official mandated the amount of soda you could drink. Reactance can reflect a false cause. For example, you are prediabetic and tune out health information because the message threatens your freedom and desire for ice-cream.

Reactance anger can arise when an agency threatens to abolish your freedoms (Rosenberg and Siegel 2018). Consider the following examples:

- You live in a community with a homeowner's association, governed by people with a dire need to control and to suppress. If you are the subject of these practices, you are likely to experience reactance anger.

- The representatives in the Rhode Island state legislature created high-sounding consumer protection laws but inserted obstacles that make it difficult for fraud victims to obtain justice through the courts (Carter 2009, 17). Denial of rights is a common source of discouragement and reactance anger.

- New Hampshire's Right to Know Law (also known as the sunshine law) gives the public direct access to public documents. Because of weaknesses in the law, many municipalities take advantage of the gaps to cloak what they do in secrecy by obstructing access to information. This unfair practice keeps the New Hampshire sunshine law under a dark cloud, leading to reactance anger among affected New Hampshire residents. (https://righttoknownh.wordpress.com/)

Third-party reactance to unfairness is a potential anger factor. You may not have been aware of some unfair practices, such as when government officials wrongly block citizens from access to information everyone has a right to know. When you discover a previously unnoticed wrong, you may experience reactance anger. Unfortunately, even when unfair practices are known, they may not hit home unless they are in plain sight, such as child abuse and the exploitation of disabled individuals.

If you have a pet peeve about an abusive practice, consider affiliating with an advocacy group of like-minded people seeking ways to make a system fair. That's a constructive way to direct a natural anger against adverse inequities.

MY PROGRESS LOG

Key ideas: What three ideas did you pick up from this chapter that you found most helpful?

1.

2.

3.

Action plan: What three steps would you take to move closer to overcoming anger excesses?

1.

2.

3.

Execution: What are you going to do to execute the steps? (The process)

1.

2.

3.

Results: What do you hope to learn—or have reinforced—by taking these steps?

1.

2.

3.

Revisions: If you would make changes in the process, what would you do differently next time?

1.

2.

3.

CHAPTER 6

Body-Mind Solutions

You awaken in a bad mood. Your mind automatically seeks a cause. Your favorite sports team lost because of a bad officiating call. That must be the reason. Or it must be that angry encounter with the hardware clerk last week. As you dwell on what you assume was the cause, your level of agitation rises. You are in a stress-anger-stress cycle.

When your body feels stressed, this unpleasant sensation is an activating event that can trigger angry thoughts. When your body feels relaxed, your mind goes along with how you feel. In this chapter we'll look at how to calm the body to promote realistically positive thoughts and break the cycle. Specifically, we'll explore

- the stress-anger-stress cycle, including ways to use stress as an early warning signal and ways to reduce anger by lowering your stress index;

- strategies for calming the body: scenes for serenity, progressive muscle relaxation, and deep breathing;

- how to improve sleep quality to reduce risks for needless stress and anger; and

- how to combat anger factors associated with coronary heart disease.

THE STRESS-ANGER-STRESS CYCLE

You'll travel on many emotive highways. Some lead to Anxietyville. Some go to Happy Point. You'll find a road to Sad Town marked on the map as well. Some are highways to Anger Villages, where each subdivision has distinctive features.

If you have figuratively taken up residence in Anger Villages, your stress tolerance is low. It doesn't take much to set you off. Your mind automatically turns to blame and condemning others for the stress that you experience. You keep going on with this process until you lessen or end the cycle.

In the Stress-Anger-Stress Village subdivision, you move along on two sides of the road at the same time. On the biology side, unpleasant sensations trigger anger thinking. At first, you might think the cause for the sensation is outside of yourself: you had an unpleasant encounter with a stranger last week. But are you barking up the wrong tree? Perhaps your chemistry is off because of a night of lousy sleep. Perhaps you are hungry, as anger is a common byproduct of hunger (MacCormack and Lindquist 2019). Or maybe you are at a low point in a circadian cycle.

In your subdivision, negative physical feelings activate negative thinking. That puts you partially on the biological side of the road, and partially on the cognitive side. When stressed, your biology can trigger anger thinking. You orient your attention toward an external source. Almost anyone will do. Your mate is stupid; that's why you feel angry. If your mate were smart, you wouldn't feel angry.

Here is what is going on. You've unintentionally layered a problem onto a problem. Your explanation for a stressed feeling prompts more stress, feeding a stress-anger-stress cycle. By pinning down the trigger for a biological stress signal, you can use this information to break the cycle. A good night's sleep, eating adequately, moderate aerobic exercise, and accepting unexplained negative sensations as transient lower the risk of amplifying stress by externalizing blame.

Affect labeling (chapter 1) and cognitive reappraisal (chapter 2) can also help. If you experience stress before you experience anger, label the sensation: "stress." You can go one step further. Identify the biological source for the anger, such as missing a meal or lacking sleep. Your biology can change when you are under a lot of stress on the job. That gives you another angle on cognitive reappraisal.

When you experience anger over stress, label the feeling "anger over stress." This can calm your amygdala by promoting a change in perspective.

Stress Rising

Based on surveys from the American Psychological Association (APA), stress has risen in the US for over ten years and has recently leveled off at a high level. The APA annually sponsors a Stress in America survey. In the 2017 survey, 80% of respondents reported at least one significant stress event in the month before the survey. On average, people said that their stress level was 5.1 on a 10-point scale, where 1 = "little or no stress" and 10 = "a great deal of stress." Thirty-five percent of the respondents reported feeling irritated or angered, and 45% reported sleep problems (APA 2017). These numbers are red flags.

Using 1 = "little to no stress" and 10 = "extremely stressed," how do you rate yourself on your stress level over the previous month? In the box below, record your rating. What are the causes?

Stress Level (1–10)	Causes

Is your stress level worth monitoring? It might be if you rate your stress as higher than 4 and persistent. Persistent or chronic stress is likely to raise your risk for stress-anger-stress cycles, interfere with quality social relationships, decrease your sense of emotional well-being, aggravate current health problems, and increase your risk for future ones.

Your Stress Glass

In the following picture, the liquid in the glasses represents general stress levels. When the glass overflows, stress transforms into a reaction, usually anger. Which of the three glasses comes closest to your current stress level?

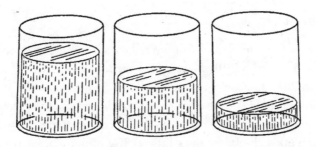

If the glass on the left seems like you, you may dwell more than what's reasonable on events that displease you. You may magnify problems and make them worse. Adding anger thoughts to the glass would be like adding an entire tray of ice cubes. It would overflow.

If the middle glass resonates with you, you probably have more stress than you'd like, but you have enough resiliency to bounce back sooner than later. A challenge is to keep matters in perspective without making more than is there.

Because you have plenty of room in the right-side glass, you have more space to absorb extra frustrations and stresses. You are in one of those rich-get-richer situations. You feel less of a need to protect yourself from stress. Paradoxically, you are likely to manage situations more effectively, get better results, and have less stress to deal with later.

Fill in your general stress-anger level in the glasses below. In the glass to the left, mark where you are now. In the middle glass, mark where you'd like your stress level to be two months from now. On the glass to your right, mark where you'd like it to be six months from now. See if having a visual goal helps.

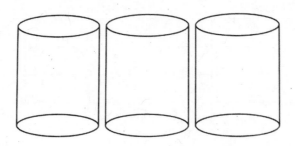

Here's the good part. Whatever glass most represents your stress-anger level now, you don't have to add torrid angry thoughts about real or imagined events. Once you see through parasitic thoughts (as you might see through a clear glass), you get to choose a different optic.

CALMING THE BODY

A calm body reflects the workings of a calm mind, and vice versa. By calming your body, you can calm your mind and experience less stress from parasitic anger. Scenes for serenity, progressive muscle relaxation, and deep breathing can help calm the body and then the mind.

Scenes for Serenity

Exposure to nature scenes can stimulate the brain, reduce stress, and help lessen the effects of stress on the body (Twedt, Rainey, and Proffitt 2019). Those who benefit the most are those who need to lower stress the most (Beute and de Kort 2018). Serene nature scenes that help promote calm have the following features: (1) blue skies, (2) green fields, (3) water, (4) no signs of human clutter, and (5) a sense that you are looking out at the scene as if you are in a sheltered place. You can find scenes for serenity in a photo or painting or by imagining (or actually being in) such places. In as little as five minutes a day, viewing a serenity scene can reduce stress and convey health benefits.

Here is an experiment. Over the next seven days, spend at least five minutes a day viewing a serene scene. After experimenting with the scenes, take stock of your level of stress. Do you notice a difference?

Following each observation of the scene for serenity, check the box that comes closest to your impression of your stress level: 1 = "calm" and 7 = "high stress".

STRESS LEVEL

DAY	1	2	3	4	5	6	7
1							
2							
3							
4							
5							
6							
7							

Use the scale as a rough measure of whether this technique works for you.

If you notice a positive difference, take this experiment one step further. What did you learn from your scenes for serenity experiment? Here is an example:

Learn
I learned that I could be consistent with viewing a serene scene each day for five minutes or more.
I can—and have already started—to step back when I start to feel angry and think about how I would think with a serene mind.

Now it's your turn to describe what you learned after your seven-day experiment.

Learn

Soothing music and nature sounds, such as the sound of a stream rolling over rocks with birds chirping in the background, can also help lower negative emotional arousal (Yu et al. 2018).

Progressive Muscle Relaxation

You can't be both relaxed and tense at the same time. That is because different nervous systems govern tension and relaxation. The *sympathetic system* mobilizes for fight and flight. The *parasympathetic system* controls rest and digestion.

American physician Edmund Jackobson (1938) mapped a muscle relaxation method for activating the parasympathetic system to reduce tension, and behavior therapist Joseph Wolpe (1973) modified the method to reduce anxiety. Progressive muscle relaxation enjoys scientific support in reducing emotional arousal (Vergara 2020), creating a sense of calm (Stevens et al. 2007), reducing stress (Gao et al. 2018), and improving sleep (Alexandru et al. 2009).

People usually do progressive muscle relaxation in a comfortable, distraction-free place on an easy chair or lying on a couch. Here's how. In an organized sequence, you tighten (without straining) and relax one major muscle group at a time. I have found it effective to take about four seconds to tighten and four to relax the tension in each of the muscle groups. There are twenty-five muscle contractions and relaxations in the sequence below. The process will take about three and a half minutes.

The eight-second cycle for each muscle group has a secondary purpose: to combine muscle relaxation with a deep-breathing exercise for an added effect. We'll discuss the deep-breathing technique shortly.

You can download the following exercise at http://www.newharbinger.com/44321.

MY PROGRESSIVE RELAXATION EXPERIMENT

There is no one right order for contracting and relaxing muscle groups. You can start with your face and work down toward your toes, reverse this sequence, or create another order. The important thing is to follow a routine pattern.

The more relaxing effects come from tensing and relaxing facial and neck muscles. Let's start with the face.

- Wrinkle your forehead. Let your forehead muscles relax.

- Make a grinning face like a Cheshire cat. Let your cheek muscles relax.

- Frown by tightening your lips downward. Let your lip muscles go limp.

- Tighten your jaw. Let your jaw muscles relax.

- Close your eyes until they are tight. Let your eyelids relax.

- Press your tongue against the roof of your mouth. Let your tongue relax.

- Pull your head gently forward until your chin touches your chest. Let your neck muscles relax.

- Move your head back. Let your neck muscles relax.

- Move your head to the right. Let your neck muscles relax.

- Move your head to the left. Let your neck muscles relax.

- Tighten your hands into fists. Let your hand muscles relax.

- Turn your wrists down and tighten your forearms. Let your wrists and forearms relax.

- Tighten your biceps. Let your biceps muscles relax.

- Stretch out your arms to tighten your triceps. Let your triceps muscles relax.

- Shrug your shoulders to tighten them. Let your shoulder muscles relax.

- Pull your shoulders back. Let your shoulder muscles relax.

- Pull your shoulders forward. Let your shoulder muscles relax.

- Arch your back to make it feel tense. Let your back muscles relax.

- Tighten your chest muscles. Let your chest muscles relax.

- Push your stomach out like a potbelly. Let your stomach muscles relax.

- Pull your stomach inward. Let your stomach muscles relax.

- Tighten your buttocks. Let your buttock muscles relax.

- Tighten your thighs. Let your thigh muscles relax.

- Tighten your calf muscles by pointing your toes forward. Let your calf muscles relax.

- Tighten your shin muscles by pointing your toes up. Let your shin muscles relax.

Deep Breathing

Deep breathing is a research-supported CBT method that can calm the mind and body by activating the parasympathetic nervous system. Deep breathing is associated with biological measures for relaxation, positive moods, and less stress (Perciavalle et al. 2017). This relaxed state is associated with improved decision making (De Couck et al. 2019).

Deep breathing doesn't solve problems. The process sets the stage for clear thinking and can serve as a distancing technique.

Top Tip: Breathe Your Way to a Clear Mind

Joel Block, PhD, ABBP, is a Long Island, New York, psychologist and author of twenty-one books, including *The 15-Minute Relationship Fix: A Clinically Proven Strategy That Will Repair and Strengthen Your Love Life* (Block 2018). He gives deep breathing as his top anger tip.

When you hold your breath, carbon dioxide builds up in the blood for a calming effect. When you breathe in, your breathing can activate your parasympathetic nervous system, calming the body and the mind.

Let's give calmness a boost. Find a comfortable place where you have no distractions and where you can sit comfortably. Close your eyes. Loosen up by rolling your shoulders around from front to back and then from back to front. Then think the word "peace."

Here is a three-part deep-breathing plan for you:

1. Take in a full deep breath for a count of four (four seconds) until your belly expands.

2. Hold your breath for another count of four.

3. Exhale slowly to a count of four.

Repeat this three-part breathing exercise for three minutes. Do this twice a day at about the same time for two weeks. If this has a calming effect, continue.

There is nothing magical about three minutes. Some go for two minutes, others for ten. It depends on you.

If you feel angry just before doing a deep-breathing exercise, you may not experience an immediate effect. It takes time for your stress hormones to return to normal levels. Meanwhile, put yourself through the paces of a three-minute deep-breathing cycle. Wait twenty minutes. Go through the deep-breathing cycle again. See if that makes a difference.

PROMOTING RESTORATIVE SLEEP

Quality sleep is critical to performance and health. How much sleep do you need each night? About eight hours is about right (Belenky et al. 2003). You may believe that you do fine with six hours or less. However, less sleep is normally associated with weaker cognitive performances (Deak and Stickgold 2010). The brain needs to go through sleep cycles to recalibrate itself, repair itself, and consolidate memories. However, there are individual differences in what constitutes adequate sleep.

Insomnia is a common complaint. About 30% of the US population report problems with sleep, such as difficulty falling asleep, interrupted sleep, and waking up early. Daytime fatigue from insomnia is associated with increased accidents, lower performance, mood problems, feelings of being on edge and angered, and health risks if insomnia is chronic. Poor quality sleep is also associated with increases in aggressive actions (Chester and Dzierzewski 2019). For example, you may find yourself angered and arguing more than usual. Even if you lose a few hours' sleep for two nights in a row, this shortfall can lead to heightened anger and aggressive impulses the following day (Krizan and Herlache 2016; Krizan and Hisler 2019).

Insomnia has a variety of psychological and physical causes. Anxious or angry rumination at sleep time is one psychological factor. Breathing problems and frequent urination are examples of physical factors. Decreasing insomnia due to ruminations involves addressing controllable cognitive and behavioral factors that interfere with sleeping. To varying degrees, CBT approaches help combat insomnia (Bothelius et al. 2013; Friedrich and Schlarb 2018; Okajima and Inoue 2018). By experimenting with different CBT sleep techniques and finding what works best for you, you can make good strides in improving your sleep patterns.

Sleep-Promoting Strategies

Let's look at seventeen cognitive, emotive, and behavioral techniques to address insomnia that you can follow as a program.

1. Follow a regular sleep schedule. Go to bed when you are likely to feel sleepy.

2. Try white noise, such as low-volume sound from a nonoperating television channel, to muffle outside sounds. (Put on the TV timer so that the set shuts off, say, in sixty minutes.)

3. If you work with a computer at night, turn on the night light option. Preliminary "iffy" evidence suggests that this blue light filtration measure can aid sleep.

4. Avoid associating your bed with wakefulness. When you are unable to sleep, get out of bed. Walk around. Quickly turn a light on and off several times. Return to bed in a few minutes. You may feel more ready to sleep.

5. If you wake up and have trouble falling back to sleep, half-fill a cup with milk. Pour in a little honey to slightly sweeten the milk. Microwave the combination to warm. Within about a half-hour after drinking this combination, you may doze off.

6. Engage in moderate aerobic exercise in the afternoon to aid sleep. (Most sleep experts suggest avoiding exercise two to four hours before you go to bed.) In a study of over 600,000 adults, moderate exercise seemed to reduce negative thinking that could impede sleep (McIntyre et al. 2020).

7. Avoid eating or drinking caffeinated substances (e.g., coffee, cola, tea, chocolate) seven hours before your regular bedtime.

8. If you smoke, refrain from doing so several hours before going to bed. (Because of proven coronary and cancer health risks, it is a good idea to struggle to kick a smoking addiction.)

9. Avoid alcohol for three hours before going to bed. A glass of wine in the evening may cause you to feel relaxed, and you may fall asleep quicker. However, as your body breaks down alcohol, you compromise the quality of your sleep. Quality is more important than quantity.

10. Sleep in a well-ventilated room with the room temperature in the sixty-eight degrees Fahrenheit range. Sleep is associated with a drop in body temperature. By dropping the ambient room temperature, you assist your sleep.

11. During periods of interrupted sleep, try deep breathing, progressive muscle relaxation, or a combination of both. To get your mind off negative thoughts, imagine a fluffy cloud moving slowly across the sky.

12. Plan to rise between 6:00 a.m. and 7:00 a.m. (There is some evidence that sleeping late increases the risk of depression, which, in turn, affects sleep.)

13. If your mind races with negative cognitions, try counting backward from one thousand by threes. As an alternative, think of something positive for each negative thought.

14. Close your eyes naturally and keep them lightly shut. Attend to the changing shadow images as you breathe deeply for two minutes.

15. When blame thinking disrupts your sleep, take a few minutes to practice cognitive reappraisal and acceptance, and consider what is in your enlightened interest to do. Keep a pad by your bed. Jot down a few ideas and put the pad aside.

16. If you awaken about two to three hours before you'd like to awaken, and you know yourself well enough to know you won't fall back to sleep, get up and do something productive. Just in case, lay something out the night before.

17. Avoid napping during the day. Keep yourself occupied until the time when you've scheduled yourself to go to bed. That is another way to get yourself into a positive sleep cycle.

The Pink Elephant Problem

It's hard to fall asleep when your mind and emotions churn with angry thoughts. You may add a layer of difficulty falling asleep when you command yourself to sleep. If you tell yourself something like *I must fall asleep. I must fall asleep*, you are less likely to fall asleep. Then you tell yourself that you must stop thinking that way or you'll stay awake. Welcome to the pink elephant problem. The harder you figuratively clench your fists to forget the elephant, the more likely the elephant will stay in mind.

To help yourself past the dilemma, imagine three words like "I must sleep" as composed of small wooden letters spreading apart and drifting in a receding tide. Imagine the letters bobbing in the water.

Relieving the early stress part of the stress-anger-stress cycle has multiple other benefits. A relaxed body and adequate quality sleep can raise your threshold for stress by lowering your stress glass level.

Combined Body-Calming Methods

To improve sleep quality, try combining progressive muscle relaxation with deep breathing before going to sleep. While lying in bed, complete the following steps:

1. As you contract a muscle group for four seconds, breathe in and fill your lungs.

2. Keep the muscle group contracted as you hold your breath for four seconds.

3. Slowly release the muscle tension to the count of four as you slowly exhale.

4. Allow your muscles to stay loose for four seconds and hold your breath at the same time.

Restart the cycle by contracting another muscle group while breathing in to fill your lungs. Continue this combination until you have completed your progressive muscle relaxation exercise.

CALMING AN ANGRY HEART

There is a potential health benefit from making use of multiple relaxation interventions to increase your resilience for stress. Anger is a common response, as well as a contributor, to stress. By increasing your stress threshold, you'll have less stress. By progressively mastering ways to reduce the biologically jarring effects of persistent forms of anger and hostility, you may find yourself experiencing that sometimes elusive feeling of confident composure.

The research on the relationship between anger and hostility as a risk factor for coronary heart disease (CHD) is compelling and has been for decades. However, people's CHD risk varies by ongoing environmental conditions and relevant biological factors. Thus, you might be high on the anger scale, go through your day with enough anger that most people stay clear of you, and live to over 100. If you are one of those rare people with great longevity genes, you might beat the odds.

When you are combatting excess anger to lower your stress, enjoy quality relationships with others, and have fewer needless anger-related problems, you are doing yourself another favor. Reducing the parasitic anger factor is a probable health booster, as you'll see below.

The Allostatic Overload Factor in CHD

When confronted with an external threat to your body and life, your brain stabilizes your body to adapt rapidly to the change. Protective discharges of hormones give you an energy boost and protect your body from externally caused damage. Inflammation protects against infection should you sustain a wound. For the most part, your biological threat responses are short-lived and disperse when you are safe.

The word "allostasis" describes this protective process of "providing enough energy to cope with any challenge—not just the life-threatening ones" (McEwen and Lasley 2002, 7). Allostasis provides increased stress hormones in the morning to balance between morning demands and readying for action. For example, if you experience public speaking anxiety, allostasis kicks in as you move toward speaking before a group. When angered over something trivial, allostasis mobilizes your body as if you were reading yourself to vanquish an opponent on the field of battle.

You can also experience an allostatic overload by, for example, continuing to stress yourself by replaying an argument for hours and days after the event. Allostatic overload occurs when your protective system gears up for action too often and too excessively. This same protective system now has a wearing and tearing effect on your body and adversely affects the brain. Avoiding harmful stressors, eating a healthy diet, and getting ample exercise are classical and practical ways to help bring the body back into balance.

Most stressors are social and have to do with threats to your image, ego, matters of fairness, respect, obedience to social standards, and norms. But your allostatic system doesn't know the difference between a bear and an insult. If you are overly sensitive to ego threats, where allostasis is activated by parasitic anger beliefs, you run the risk of an allostatic overload.

Allostatic overload happens when you overcharge your body too often as a result of the stress-anger-stress cycle. As we discussed earlier, this is caused by frequently recurring anger episodes or recurring angry thoughts and feelings (e.g., those that occur when working in a hostile environment).

Over time, allostatic overload raises your risk for disease (McEwen and Rasgon 2018). If you are prone to anger or hostility, you risk overloading your vascular system and heart with stress hormones (Chida and Steptoe 2009; Williams et al. 2000). The overload includes C-reactive protein that triggers inflammation, which some scientists suggest contributes to clogged arteries and cardiovascular disease. Anger patterns are also risk factors for degrading your immune system (Janicki-Deverts, Cohen, and Doyle 2010) and diminishing your pulmonary (lung) functioning (Kubzansky et al. 2006).

Anger Factors Affecting the Heart—and Solutions

A relaxed body and mind buffer you from overly active angry and hostile thoughts and actions. By spending less time with angry and hostile cognitions, you'll have more time for living with a relaxed mind and body.

The following chart shows anger factors that, when ongoing, could contribute to CHD through an allostatic overload state. By knowing what to target, you can efficiently act against those anger factors. The first column describes eight different anger risk factors. You'll find descriptions in the second column, along with supporting references. The third column contains a sample solution for each.

Angry-Heart Factor	Description	Constructive Alternative
False Justifications for Anger	Blaming others for your anger (Davidson and Mostofsky 2010).	Accept responsibility for your feelings.
Anger Rumination	Going over and over the same negative, parasitic anger thoughts (Busch, Pössel, and Valentine 2017).	Imagine the thoughts floating freely into the clouds and returning to Earth as raindrops with words that splash on the ground.

Angry-Heart Factor	Description	Constructive Alternative
Negative Affect	The triple threat of anxiety, depression, and anger (Kubzansky and Kawachi 2000).	Recognize and separate each factor from the mix. Identify the parasitic cognitive signatures of each (see chapter 2). Change the signatures. Follow this divide-and-conquer approach, and you can weaken the connection between the triple threat factors.
Expressed Hostility	An attitude of ill-will expressed by telling people off, promoting suffering, etc. (Chida and Steptoe 2009; Smaardijk et al. 2020).	Determine if the belief is worth the time and effort to support it, or if you have better things to do with your life.
Suppressed Hostility	Denying and concealing hateful feelings to avoid conflict, to avoid a fear of retaliation, and by going overboard on politeness and manners to appear different from how you feel (Julkunen et al. 1994).	Avoid an accusatory tone that might invite retaliation. Instead, practice expressing thoughts flexibly, such as, "I believe" or "It seems to me, based on what I know at this time…"
Suppressed Anger	Stuffing and hiding and internalizing your anger by not expressing the emotion appropriately at the time of its occurrence. People who typically hold in anger are more likely to experience hypertension (Hosseini et al. 2011). (Temporary expression suppression is different. You recognize that a later time is a better time for a tempered response.)	Express anger feelings by referencing a specific issue. Present your feelings assertively and in a nonaccusatory, nondefensive, and nonjudgmental way.
Cynical Distrust and Pessimism	A habitual attitude of suspicion and distrust of others that, along with a wave of volatile anger, prompts unpleasant relationships and increases coronary heart disease risk (Greenglass 1996). Pessimism, a factor in cynical distrust, is associated with higher levels of inflammation, hypertension, and CHD (Roy et al. 2010).	Do voluntary work to help protect those who can't protect themselves. Cooperative work with and through others is the prime path to this goal.

Angry-Heart Factor	Description	Constructive Alternative
Proactive (Instrumental) and Related Aggressions	Repeatedly and aggressively trying to benefit at another's expense (Suarez, Lewis, and Kuhn 2002; Takahashi et al. 2018).	Do a role reversal: consider how you'd prefer others to treat you. By pausing and reflecting, you may experience the influence of your rational powers to divert the angry energy to something constructive that is of shorter duration.

Anger and hostility, in their various forms, are not the only psychological factors that contribute to CHD and other health problems. Patterns of depression and anxiety can be aversive, too, as can a pessimistic view on life.

If, after reviewing the above chart, you hear yourself saying, *That sounds like me*, you have many ways to lower your risk. All the above angry-heart factors involve negative thinking. A positive change in this area can be beneficial to your health and relationships with others. Let's practice ways to do that.

MY HEALTHY HEART PROGRAM

It is your turn to use what you have learned thus far to curb anger thinking, reduce an allostatic overload, and support heart health. Think of this experiment as a down payment on an insurance policy. In the following Heart-Healthy Program chart, cite an example that applies to your personal situation in the Angry-Heart Factor column. Next, write down a possible solution in the Constructive Alternative column.

HEART-HEALTHY PROGRAM

Angry-Heart Factor	Description	Constructive Alternative
False Justifications for Anger		

Angry-Heart Factor	Description	Constructive Alternative
Anger Rumination		
Negative Affect		
Expressed Hostility		
Suppressed Hostility		
Suppressed Anger		

Angry-Heart Factor	Description	Constructive Alternative
Cynical Distrust and Pessimism		
Proactive (Instrumental) and Related Aggressions		

What did you learn from the experiment that you might pass on to a friend with an anger problem?

As you continue to read through the book, look for concepts and exercises that apply to this area that work for you. Return to the Heart-Healthy Program chart as many times as you choose. You can download the chart at http://www.newharbinger.com/44321 and print a copy. Add ideas about what you believe you can do to reduce anger-related health risks and improve your social and personal lifestyle choices.

The foremost authority on allostasis, Rockefeller University professor Bruce McEwen, suggests using mindfulness methods to stop ruminating about things you cannot change. Mindfulness practices reduce internal stress and the resulting allostatic load and facilitate the positive aspects of your life ("count your blessings!").

Top Tip: Mindfulness Methods

Mindfulness is an "in-the-moment" experience. You exist in the present moment and in no other time. Mindfulness refers to a variety of accepting, nonjudgmental ways to attend to present-moment experiences to promote a relaxed mind, calm body, and emotional well-being. Emory University assistant professor of medicine, Dr. William Knaus, MD (not to be confused with the author of this workbook), suggests four ways to do this.

First, here are two scientifically tested mindfulness techniques for lowering general stress and promoting a sense of well-being:

Mantra meditation. For five minutes daily, silently repeat a word like *One* or a sound like *Hummm* (the mantra) as you deeply breathe. If you get distracted, come back to the mantra. It takes about six weeks to start benefitting.

Body scanning. University of Massachusetts professor Jon Kabat-Zinn (2005) describes the power of the mind to release physical and psychological tension:

> *Without moving a muscle, we can put our mind anywhere in the body we choose and feel and be aware of whatever sensations are present at the moment.* (Kabat-Zinn, 383)

You systematically mentally scan different parts of your body, from your toes to the top of your head. For each body region, you tune into your sensations of warmth, tension, tingling, or others. Then you combine all areas into the whole of you. The Internet is rich in body scan examples. (Note: You can scan the muscles listed under "Progressive Muscle Relaxation" above for this body scanning exercise. You can add deep breathing to each part you scan.) Try body scanning once a day for eight weeks and see if you anger yourself less often.

Second, here are two brief mindfulness imagery techniques to test to see if they help interrupt the flow of negative thoughts that can lead to allostatic overload:

The flight of angry thoughts technique. Anger thoughts connect the meaning of a situation to aroused anger feelings. To help yourself break this thought connection, imagine your angry thoughts dispersing through fluffy clouds. Hold the image for two minutes.

The cuteness technique. When you imagine a cute animal, what comes to mind first? Is it a puppy, kitten, koala bear, or something else? When you arise in the morning, and when you go to bed at night, for a minute, imagine your animal's face.

Choosing Optimism over Pessimism

Pessimism is related to coronary health problems (Felt et al. 2020), whereas optimism is correlated with longevity (Lee et al. 2019).

Even an unrealistic optimism, where you anticipate that negative events occurring in the present moment will change for the better in the future, is probably a healthier view compared to a situation where you have a realistic pessimism that something will go wrong and then ruminate about that.

Realistic optimism is a practical form of optimism. You accept that some actions by some will sometimes displease you. At the same time, you are free to command yourself and the controllable events around you. You have confidence in your ability to shape the controllable parts of your future. This means you have rational choices, including the Stoic choice of knowing that events don't dictate how you *must* think.

MY PROGRESS LOG

Key ideas: What three ideas did you pick up from this chapter that you found most helpful?

1.

2.

3.

Action plan: What three steps would you take to move closer to overcoming anger excesses?

1.

2.

3.

Execution: What are you going to do to execute the steps? (The process)

1.

2.

3.

Results: What do you hope to learn—or have reinforced—by taking these steps?

1.

2.

3.

Revisions: If you would make changes in the process, what would you do differently next time?

1.

2.

3.

CHAPTER 7

The Frustration-Tension
Tolerance Solution

Feelings of frustration and other tensions are signals that something is off-kilter—an unpleasant warning of sorts. That's a natural signal. But an intolerance for tension is a horse of a different color. This is an unwillingness to tolerate discomfort, negative emotions, and conditions of uncertainty. When someone is intolerant of tension, they either magnify the feeling they find unacceptable or discharge it impulsively.

A low tolerance for tension is at the core of much human misery. It's like being in a revolving door where each new unpleasant event triggers a whole new round of negative thoughts and feelings. For example, you may feel anger more often with a low tolerance for frustration (Mahon et al. 2006).

You can lower your risk for parasitic anger by building high frustration or tension tolerance. You'll have fewer self-inflicted stresses and strains in your life. Together we'll map a path toward building high frustration and tension tolerance skills you can use daily to feel more comfortable with yourself and lessen anger excesses. The points of interest on this map include

- recognizing the feeling of tension as a common anger trigger in order to decrease anger stimulated by this core process,

- understanding the connection between anger and low frustration tolerance,

- breaking the cycle of anger catastrophizing,

- avoiding double trouble anger incidents, and

- building high frustration tolerance to lower your general level of tension.

This part of the map may be the most important waypoint on your self-mastery journey. With fewer negative sensations, you are likely to have fewer causes for parasitic anger thinking and aggressive reactions.

THE TENSION-ANGER SPINOFF EFFECT

Anger thoughts and unpleasant sensations feed off of each other. If you are prone to think angry thoughts, you'll feel it in your gut. If you feel negative sensations, these sensations increase your risk for angry thoughts (Berkowitz 1990; Knaus 1982). Label this the *tension-anger spinoff effect*, and you may be less susceptible to it.

A low tolerance for tension increases your vulnerability for anger. Suppose one day you wake up with a vague unpleasant feeling. You don't know why. If you are like many others, you'll go in search of a cause. It usually doesn't take long to find one. Maybe the feeling reminds you of a rude comment your boss made yesterday. Now you know why you feel anger. However, it is also possible that your unpleasant feeling had nothing to do with your boss or anybody else. You've created a fiction to explain an unpleasant feeling that first appeared unattached to anything else—like it came from out of the blue. Another common trigger for anger is frustration, which I'll cover next.

ANGER AND LOW FRUSTRATION TOLERANCE

It's natural to feel frustration when you come to a barrier between where you are and where you want to be. Your car won't start. You're behind on a deadline. Your partner keeps interrupting you when you are trying to concentrate on a project. Of course, some things matter more than others do. You are at risk of losing a friendship over a silly argument. You fail an entry examination for your chosen profession. Maybe you can save the friendship. You can reapply for the examination and study with a group as opposed to studying alone as before.

Frustration isn't a problem when it's proportional to a situation. Frustration motivates problem solving and other actions to rectify wrongs, defend against unfair practices, and promote socially sensible actions. Proportion is normally in your enlightened self-interest, whereas overplaying a situation is ordinarily not.

Low frustration tolerance (LFT) is a problem when you experience extraordinary difficulties tolerating unpleasant feelings, inconveniences, hassles, and situations you don't want to experience. When you have a pileup of LFT within a relatively short time, your stress glass from chapter 6 fills fast.

LFT is a trigger for many forms of emotional distresses and especially for excess anger and aggression. If you have a short trigger for reacting and thinking in response to frustration, you are likely to magnify the onerousness of situations with negative thoughts. In chapter 2 we learned about *cognitive signatures*—predictable lines of thought that go with negative mood states like anger. Here is a common cognitive signature: "I can't stand it." Typically, the "it" refers to the tension you feel. Low frustration self-talk (i.e., internal chatter) includes *This is too much*.

If you find yourself in an LFT cycle, your awareness of how you magnify situations is an important step to set yourself free from the pattern. Let's see how to recognize and deal with this LFT magnification process.

ANGER CATASTROPHIZING

Some situations are catastrophic for objective reasons. Learning you have a terminal illness is catastrophic. Losing your home in a fire or tornado is a catastrophe regarding the implications of the loss. Catastrophizing is different. *Catastrophizing* is blowing things out of proportion and making past, present, or possible future events far worse than they are. Psychologist Albert Ellis is best known for coining and defining the word "catastrophizing." Earlier, psychiatrist Tom Williams called this "calamity-howling" (Williams 1923, 106).

Combine a down mood, unpleasant event, and parasitic anger belief(s), and you have a triple threat condition for *anger catastrophizing*. Figuratively, this is a whipped-up mental whirlwind of exaggerating the significance of a situation by complaining, blaming, and escalating tensions, triggering more negative thinking. For example, you bring friends to the zoo to see a new giraffe. You get there and see this sign: "Closed for Renovations." You blow up the situation (figuratively) into an end-of-life calamity. You extend blame and condemn zoo management for not advertising the closing where you could see it. You think, *Those clowns who run this place are idiots and should all lose their jobs.* (Extensions of blame are a common part of anger catastrophizing.) You continue with a blaming, complaining tirade and turn a disappointment into the equivalent of a 100-mile-wide meteor heading to Earth with no way to stop it.

Albert Ellis (1999) coined another word, *awfulizing*, to describe a process that often accompanies catastrophizing. According to Ellis, awfulizing is not only blowing something out of proportion, but also making an unpleasant and difficult event into something horrible and beyond the ability of any human to tolerate. It's worse than 100% bad! Like catastrophizing, awfulizing has roots in LFT. Awfulizing and LFT are related to hostile thoughts (Martin and Dahlen 2004).

Here is an example of where LFT is an undercurrent for anger catastrophizing flavored with awfulizing:

Linda and her closest high school classmates planned to meet for their annual reunion at their favorite restaurant. She left early to make sure she'd be there on time. She decided to drive her husband's classic sports car, maybe to show off a little bit.

Roaring down the highway with her hair flowing in the wind, Linda felt excited. That changed fast. She braked for stalled traffic. After about ten minutes without moving, Linda realized she was going to be late. She felt a strong surge of frustration. She angrily told herself, Some idiot got into an accident. Come on. Come on. Get the wreck off the road.

Linda amplified her anger with blame thinking. She blamed an unknown driver for screwing up her schedule. She blamed the state troopers for not directing traffic around the wreck. She told herself, This should not be. Fools run this state.

The more Linda thought about her situation, the more she saw her inconvenience as awful. She catastrophized about that as well. As her frustrations and anger escalated, she upset herself for feeling distressed. She pulled her cell phone out of her purse to tell her friends she'd be late. Alas. The battery was dead. Her charger was in her regular car. She screamed, pounded the steering wheel, and honked the horn.

In this example, LFT and anger catastrophizing play out this way:

1. Experience a situation as frustrating when you cannot get or do what you want.

2. Target someone or something to blame.

3. Exaggerate the onerousness of the situation by doing something like (1) proclaiming, "This should not be"; (2) demanding, "I must have my way"; (3) extending blame, such as, "The creeps who did this should go down hard"; and (4) feeling high distress fueled by these extra mental machinations, continuing to magnify the situation.

4. Vent your anger to discharge the tension by verbally or physically striking out or by suppressing aggression when you think you are in a vulnerable position.

Linda prepared herself to end her tendency to anger catastrophize before the process got out of hand. She focused on the frustration tolerance angle to figuratively pull the props out from under anger catastrophizing.

Linda used the following chart to compare her low frustration tolerance response to the situation involving the traffic tie-up and an alternative high frustration tolerance view. The first column describes a general low frustration tolerance and anger-catastrophizing process. The second column gives an example of how Linda engaged that process. The third column shows a radical change from the pattern.

If your frustration tolerance is naturally low, it may be especially difficult for you to choose to take a high frustration tolerance view. However, knowledge is power. If you know what you are up against, you have choices. The idea behind column three is simple: if you can see a better option, you have the freedom to take it. Here are Linda's responses:

Low Frustration Tolerance–Anger-Catastrophizing Process	Low Frustration Tolerance Response	Alternative High Frustration Tolerance View
You view a situation as frustrating when you cannot get or do what you want.	Linda saw the situation as inconvenient, intolerable, horrible, and one that "should not be."	Linda saw the situation as frustrating, undesirable, and a problem.
You view and define the situation as unbearably onerous and catastrophize by internally ranting about how awful the situation is and how foul and condemnable the culprits are. This exaggeration continues.	Linda amplified her tension by fixing her attention on the situation and her negative thoughts about the traffic tie-up.	Linda focused her attention on what she could control, which was to start reading a novel by her favorite author while listening to flute music on a CD.
You target someone or something to blame, and then extend the blame into damning and condemning.	Linda blamed and condemned the drivers, tow truck operators, state police, and state government for the delay.	Blaming and condemning doesn't change an impossible situation. Acceptance of adversity brought her frustration to a lower level.
You focus your attention on the feeling, magnify it, act as if you can't tolerate what you feel, and experience a strong urgency to discharge the tension.	Linda's frustration and anger intensity were high. She focused her attention on her feelings and blamed others for ruining her good mood. She overfocused on how rotten she felt.	Linda accepted responsibility for amplifying her intolerance. She recognized that how she defined the situation (horrible, blameworthy) influenced how she interpreted the situation beyond the normal and expected levels for the situation. It was out of proportion.
You verbally or physically strike out.	Linda's anger catastrophizing took the form of pounding the steering wheel and honking the horn.	By defusing anger catastrophizing, you eliminate that specious temporary relief reward that, in turn, reinforces anger catastrophizing, making this pattern more likely to return. That's a big plus!

If you find yourself in an anger-catastrophizing trap, the following comparison experiment will help you extricate yourself from that process.

AN EXPERIMENT IN COMPARISONS

Think about an anger-catastrophizing situation you recently experienced. In the second column, fill in your low frustration tolerance response to the catastrophizing situation. In the high frustration column, use information from this book, or other sources, that you believe will boost your frustration tolerance and increase your effectiveness in handling the next frustrating situation that you face.

Low Frustration Tolerance–Anger-Catastrophizing Process	Low Frustration Tolerance Response	Alternative High Frustration Tolerance View
You view a situation as frustrating when you cannot get or do what you want.		
You view and define the situation as unbearably onerous and catastrophize by internally ranting about how awful the situation is and how foul and condemnable the culprits are. This exaggeration continues.		
You target someone or something to blame, and then extend the blame into damning and condemning.		
You focus your attention on the feeling, magnify it, act as if you can't tolerate what you feel, and experience a strong urgency to discharge the tension.		
You verbally or physically strike out.		

You are on your way to being a decatastrophizing expert when you conclude, *I don't like the situation. I don't like feeling frustrated. I don't like catastrophizing. I can stand what I don't like. I can calmly work to self-improve.*

DITCH DOUBLE TROUBLES

You can't stop thinking about a recent affront. Your tension rises. You need to relax and concentrate your attention on a pressing personal matter. The harder you try to stop thinking and start relaxing, the worse things get.

Distressing yourself over feeling distressed increases your risk of aggravating an already negative state. This double trouble involves layering an unnecessary secondary problem upon a problem, such as frustrating yourself over feeling frustrated or angering yourself over feeling angry. Self-statements such as *I can't stand this* often amplify tension. Look for these secondary distresses when you feel a desperation to feel free of distress.

If you make too much of real or imagined troublesome events and you anger catastrophize, you've double troubled yourself by blaming and complaining. You now have the original situation and the lingering after-effects. When you add LFT thinking, you pile on an extra layer of misery. You double trouble yourself over the distress. You feel worse. That's a big trouble, but one you can get out of.

Double troubles are a great area to target when this applies to you. There is so much you can do to reduce or rid yourself of self-inflicted burdens that are often worse than the original one. Following are some helpful strategies.

Label your "double trouble." You can address anger catastrophizing when you see it as a double trouble, but not when you don't. By knowing that anger catastrophizing doubles your trouble, you can reduce the urgency of that moment and discharge the tension. Use this knowledge as an early warning signal to take quick corrective action.

Accept troubling thoughts. If you accept that you grow more upset from magnifying the significance of an event and you believe you can find a way to squeeze the excesses from that thinking, give yourself a progress point.

Isolate parasitic anger thinking. You may blow even a tragic loss out of proportion and anger yourself excessively. Keeping the event in perspective doesn't diminish the loss. Anger catastrophizing does! To break the cycle, start by separating the natural meaning of a loss from the double troubles caused by catastrophizing. You are likely to experience a natural feeling about the type of loss and have freedom from parasitic exaggerations.

Consider a need for importance. You might anger catastrophize when you experience an irrational need for power slipping away, and then double up on your trouble. This double trouble can be an offshoot of believing that you must be in control to feel important. If you parasitically anger yourself in this way, try to double-down on the double trouble by evoking acceptance as a strategy. Remember, you don't have to be 100% important to feel confident.

Think about your thinking. When is your thinking an anger accelerant? Do thoughts like *I can't stand this, and I will harm someone* amplify your anger? If so, deescalate the language. Instead of allowing thoughts like *I can't take this anymore*, describe the event in concrete terms, such as, *I'm stalled in traffic, and I don't like it.*

BUILD HIGH FRUSTRATION TOLERANCE

Is it possible to take an organized approach to reduce your parasitic thinking and decrease your tension? Below are two methods to help you do this: the body, mind, patterns, and connections approach, and the PURRRRS technique.

Body, Mind, Patterns, and Connections

This is a four-step approach to reducing tension and frustration.

1. *Build the body* to lessen physical tension. Quality sleep, exercise, and calorie-restricted diets contribute to this end and normally improve the quality of your thinking, which, in turn can aid sleep. Thus, a healthy body and mind is a bidirectional process where each influences the other. There is a research trend showing exercise having a slight benefit on sleep (Kline 2019). For example, moderate aerobic exercise (e.g., walking, biking, kayaking) for thirty minutes a day may be enough to produce a positive effect on sleep quality, providing this is done earlier in the day. Exercise is also effective in reducing depression (Knaus 2012). When sufficient sleep, exercise, and healthy diet are in sync, your tolerance for tension is likely to be higher than if the opposite were so.

2. *Liberate the mind from parasitic anger thinking and repetitive negative thinking.* Rehashing angry and vengeful thoughts and frustrating yourself easily can have physical side effects, such as sleep, mood, and anger problems that can adversely affect your judgment. You can help liberate your mind by using practical, empirical, and core methods that you learned in chapter 1. Here is a tested practical solution: imagine your negative thoughts floating inside of a helium balloon, slowly drifting into the stratosphere of irrelevancy. Here is a tested empirical method: Write a script in which you reappraise a situation by judging it from different angles. From a core standpoint, consider if your human worth is dependent on perfectly controlling whatever you undertake.

3. *Change self-defeating patterns.* How do you know if a pattern is a self-defeating one? You can tell by the results. For example, if you are busy, busy, busy, and that correlates with sleep problems, look for ways to pace yourself. If you spend too much time thinking about yourself and your grievances, balance it with reasons for feeling grateful, such as that you are alive. If you repeatedly get into arguments with different people, ask yourself if you have anything to do with this. When you identify your part of the responsibility for your tension, you are on your way to changing the pattern.

4. *Connect with supportive people* who do a better than average job of handling their frustrations. Also, identify people you can avoid who are consistently malcontented about one thing or another.

Co-ruminate with them and you may find you fuel each other's anger catastrophizing. Instead, look for ways to keep a conversation upbeat. By getting into that mindset, you may feel upbeat.

By engaging in such activities to build your frustration tolerance, you can lower your level of stress, improve your performances, train your brain to be less reactive, and improve your physical health (Tabibnia and Radecki 2018).

The PURRRRS Technique

PURRRRS is a technique for slowing down, figuring things out, and acting effectively. It is especially useful to nip anger catastrophizing in the bud. Here are the steps in this process.

Pause. You are unlikely to change a process without being aware of the process you want to change. In this awareness phase, you pause by tuning into your anger signals. You start to gather your thoughts by asking yourself what the anger signal means. Is a fast action warranted? Do you need to think before you act? If you need a reminder to ask yourself these questions, put a green dot on your thumb or your watch.

Use. This is your mobilization step. Use your resources to monitor your thinking. Put your thinking into slow motion and review what you just told yourself. This monitoring makes your thoughts accessible to examination, which occurs in the next step.

Reflect. The pause and use steps set the stage for reflecting. In this phase, expand on the issue. Gather information. Reflect on how you feel. Examine what you are telling yourself. Think deeply about what is happening to lead you to parasitic anger distractions.

Reason. In the reasoning phase, you evaluate your self-talk. What is the emotional tone of your thoughts? Does your thinking put you at the precipice of intolerance for frustration and anger and aggressive actions? If so, what do you need to do to change the trajectory? Are you developing a picture in your mind for what you'd like to accomplish and your options? What is within your power to do to lessen your tension and increase your effectiveness? What steps can you take now? The steps are the instructions that you give to yourself to follow. Look beyond the moment and estimate where following your instructions will get you.

Respond. Follow your instructions by talking yourself through the paces.

Review and revise. As conditions change, modify what you do to adapt to the changes. In ongoing situations, revisions often take place on the fly.

Stabilize. Keep practicing and improving until PURRRRS is automatic in situations where it is needed. This process will help you to recognize, evaluate, and replace low frustration tolerance, extensions of blame, and various other forms of anger thinking that can spin off from tension.

The following chart shows how to use PURRRRS. The first column describes the steps in the process. The second column describes some sample techniques. In the third column, add techniques you think will be useful. Next time you get into an anger-catastrophizing situation, in column four, record what happened at each step in the PURRRRS process.

When you become confident that you can honestly say that "tension is not terrible" and "I can live with tension," you may wonder where all the extra tension and stress in your tension glass went.

PURRRRS	Sample Actions	Your Techniques	Results
Pause and attend to what is happening.	Put a green dot on your thumbnail to remind yourself to look before you leap.		
Use personal resources to mobilize for positive action.	Distance yourself. Take a deep breath. Sit back at an angle. Take a brief walk.		
Reflect in order to figure out what is going on.	Ask yourself these questions: 1. What is the meaning of my frustration signal? 2. What needs immediate attention? What doesn't need attention? 3. Am I making too much of the situation? 4. What would the wisest person I know do in the same situation?		

Reason and plan it out. Here you start a problem-analysis and action-planning phase.	Start with these questions: 1. What is the most constructive thing I can accomplish? 2. What steps would I take first?		
Respond by putting your plan into action.	Talk yourself through the paces on a step-by-step basis (e.g., say, *I'll do this first*, then take that step). After you've taken the first step, tell yourself about how you'll start the second step, then start, and so on.		
Review and revise to improve your odds for a positive outcome.	When you find glitches in your plan, see if you can modify what you do on the spot. If you figure out a change you could make, where can you check out the modification to see if this improves the outcome?		
Stabilize by continuing to practice PURRRRS until the process is automatic.	Make practicing reasonable and effective responses a priority. In this way, you are training your brain and mind to respond proportionally.		

By regularly practicing PURRRRS, you teach yourself to substitute a reasoning process for an impulsive, anger-catastrophizing one. This will enable you to eventually prevent angering yourself for the wrong reasons.

If this part of a journey in self-mastery were easy, everyone would do it. However, if you choose this path toward tension tolerance, you'll find many ways to help yourself on this challenging journey—both in this book and elsewhere in your life.

MY PROGRESS LOG

Key ideas: What three ideas did you pick up from this chapter that you found most helpful?

1.

2.

3.

Action plan: What three steps would you take to move closer to overcoming anger excesses?

1.

2.

3.

Execution: What are you going to do to execute the steps? (The process)

1.

2.

3.

Results: What do you hope to learn—or have reinforced—by taking these steps?

1.

2.

3.

Revisions: If you would make changes in the process, what would you do differently next time?

1.

2.

3.

CHAPTER 8

Problem-Solving Solutions

What's the problem? That's a common way to start a first CBT session. Here, *problem* means what is troubling you the most. The question normally elicits an answer and back-and-forth communications leading to the discovery of core issues, resolutions, and relief.

Let's look at parasitic anger as a problem to solve. In this chapter we'll explore CBT problem-solving approaches for making positive changes. Here you'll learn

- how to define a problem as the first step in problem solving,

- a nine-step problem-solving approach to your anger problem,

- how to rewrite the parasitic anger script in your head,

- how to prevent and diminish dangerous anger outbursts, and

- how to break a shame-anger connection and avoid excess negativity.

WHAT IS A PROBLEM?

A problem exists when you have a gap between where you are and where you want to be, and that gap contains unknowns. Breaching the gap takes alterations in your thinking and actions to form new solutions. If you don't have an effective response in mind, then you'll have some thinking and experimenting to do. Sometimes this takes a studied approach.

Problem Finding

Some anger problems are symptoms of something else. For example, if you think others make you feel angry, you might also believe that your problem is to get them to stop. You might sometimes be persuasive or influential in some ways. However, the only person you can change is yourself. If you discover that parasitic anger thoughts are prompting the problem, you have found an issue you can resolve.

Problem finding is using your observational and reasoning skills to discover problems that are useful to solve. This phase comes both before and during problem solving. As you work to solve a problem, you may unearth issues you hadn't considered as part of the problem you want to solve. Here are two examples.

- You come across as angry and people back away. Your relationships are typically tense, and you feel angry when you think people don't like you. You try to figure out how to break free of this cycle. Then, you come across an eye-opening passage in a book that seems to apply to you: *You mistakenly think that others think about you as you think about yourself.* Thus, if you think negatively about yourself, so will they. With that insight, you learn to appreciate your finer qualities as you work to improve your relationships.

- You know it is wise to address conflicts before they pile up. You discover that when you focus on your feelings of discomfort, you tend to put things off. This pileup can create a sense of being overwhelmed and anger thinking about it all. You eventually feel relieved when you do address the discomfort-dodging issue, and discover that addressing conflicts sooner is less stressful. When you do this, you've solved a huge problem (a pileup) before it even starts.

NINE PROBLEM-SOLVING STEPS

"Problem solving clearly refers to the process or technique by which one attempts to 'discover' a solution to a problem" (D'Zurilla and Goldfried 1971, 109). One of the most important goals (if not the most important one) of any personal problem-solving effort is to state the problem to yourself in a clear, straightforward, and easy-to-understand way. You might start this process by telling yourself what you want to accomplish, such as, *I'd like to stop eating away at myself with my anger so I can feel calmer inside.* A second step is to expand upon the issue. For example, what do you mean about eating away at yourself inside? What do you tell yourself when you feel that way? Is there any connection? You decide your problem is to identify and change anger thinking to feel calmer inside.

Most problems have more than one workable solution, yet some solutions will be more helpful to you than others. You can't always tell which solutions will be most helpful to you without trying them out. Following are nine steps for problem finding and problem solving to keep recurring parasitic anger conditions off your back.

1. **Look at recurring stressors for *problem finding*.** Are the anger-triggering situations driven by external events? What makes this a persistent issue? Are you likely to overreact to small matters when you have slept poorly, when your mood is negative, or when you've missed a meal?

2. **Assess anger for patterns.** What do you typically do in recurring anger situations? What typically results? Does this help you predict your response?

3. **Examine how you process your observations.** What do you believe about a provocative situation? Which of those beliefs are parasitic? Once you see the parasites, you can contest them.

4. **Identify your resources for solving tough anger problems.** Do you have effective communication skills? Can you stay flexibly focused? In other words, can you adapt what you do to new information while keeping your eyes on what's important to your enlightened self-interest? How do your perceptions of your coping resources affect what you do?

5. **Give yourself a direction for meeting an achievable goal.** In simple terms, your goal is what you want to accomplish. Here are two concrete ways of stating your goals: A *mastery goal* involves learning and applying personal problem-solving skills. For example, you want to decrease parasitic anger when discussing a change in an acrimonious relationship with another. A *performance goal* is about getting a result: You want to speak with your boss about a discrepancy in salary without getting angry. When both mastery and performance goals are meaningful, measurable, and attainable, you are more likely to act to achieve them.

6. **Make a plan to achieve your goal.** Your plan is the actual steps that you'll take toward achieving your goal. If your goal is to reduce aggressive actions, then the steps might include developing distancing skills, cognitive reappraisal skills, and so on. If your goal is to improve a relationship tarnished by anger, this may take thoughtful, conciliatory steps. You decide what you think will help. Those are your steps.

7. **Take steps to implement what you planned.** Some steps are easier to do than others. Affect labeling and sitting at an angle are quick and practical. Cognitive appraisal is slower and deliberate. In situations such as trying to repair a tattered relationship, first imagine yourself taking reconciliatory steps. That's your dry run. Once in the situation, talk yourself through the steps. Plan on rewarding yourself for following the process (and adjusting as needed) with something you'd normally like to do, such as drinking a cup of coffee or watching a TV show. (Small rewards following executed actions make future implementation more likely.)

8. **Evaluate and revise to improve the change process.** The implementation of your plan may veer from what you anticipate because of unforeseen circumstances. So do a review. What seemed helpful, and what would you redo? What part of the problem can you alter?

9. **Accept that acceptance is a solution when you meet an immovable object.** Know when to write something off for now and try again when you see a change and an opportunity. You approached someone to break an acrimonious relationship cycle, and that person had no interest in a change. The idea was fine. The timing was off. Some things you have to write off.

If a friend or relative were to face the same anger problem, what advice would you give them? For example, would you suggest that when they work out steps beforehand, they take the time to visualize how they might execute them? Or that it might help to consider alternative reactions—which are unfavorable, favorable, or mixed? Would you suggest that they explore adjustments they might make? Now try to apply that same advice to yourself as you complete the next exercise.

MY PROBLEM-SOLVING EXPERIMENT

For the following experiment, pick a recurring anger problem that you think is in your enlightened self-interest to solve or resolve. Complete the following action outline as if you were advising a good friend or close family member. In the second column, describe the steps you find important based on each of your assessment factors. Then test the approach. In column three, record what resulted.

Problem-Solving Step	Action Planned	Results of Actions Taken
Look at recurring stressors for *problem finding*.		
Assess anger for patterns.		
Examine how you process your observations.		
Identify your resources for solving tough problems.		
Give yourself a direction for meeting an achievable goal.		
Make a plan to achieve your goal.		
Take steps to implement what you planned.		
Evaluate and revise to improve the change process.		
Accept that acceptance is a solution when you meet an immovable object.		

In a few days, take a second look at what you did to bring about the results. What did you learn? What would you change? Write this down below. What would you tell yourself, as if you were your own best friend?

CHANGE THE SCRIPT PROBLEM SOLUTION

The founder of personal construct therapy, psychologist George Kelly, a cognitive behavior therapy pioneer, noted that there are many successful ways that people can look at their world, and so they are not mere victims of circumstances. He found that people create theories about why they act as they do, why others act as they do, and the causes for events. They filter reality through these constructs. And when there is a distorted view about a situation, they act without awareness of the distortions (Kelly, 1955).

There is no end to the different explanations you can imagine and adopt. Some might serve you better than others. The challenge is to come up with better and better ones (Kelly 1969, 125). Kelly suggests reframing situations by experimenting with new behaviors that extend your capabilities and broaden your perspective. Although the focus of his work was on changing roles, his work can be applied to changing negative blame evaluations and exaggerations that fuel parasitic anger.

RESCRIPTING PROBLEM-SOLVING EXERCISE

Here is a modified version of Kelly's approach. Follow the steps below to see if you can create a new script and gain relief from needless parasitic anger problems.

1. Recall several incidents where anger was a disadvantageous factor. What do you recall telling yourself that was parasitic? That was your anger script.

2. What change in your thinking might help you move through life with fewer anger-related frictions?

3. Create a new script based on that change in thinking that you have reason to believe voids the problems inherent in the friction-promoting anger view. (The script needs to sound reasonable, plausible, and doable.)

4. Do a mental rehearsal test run. See how that works for you in the next step.

5. Based on the results of your new script, make modifications in your script.

6. Test the script in a future anger-trigger situation that is like the one you rehearsed. Play out the new script.

   Record the results of the experiment in the box below.

By changing the script and acting as if you could respond to the same situation without these distortions, you can create an alternative construct for yourself that works better for you than a parasitic script would.

ANGER ATTACK PROBLEM SOLUTIONS

While all anger excesses bear self-monitoring, intermittent explosive reactions (anger attacks, explosive outbursts) present a special danger. You might break objects, batter people, yell and scream, run someone off the road in a rage, or blindly do something that can lead to legal troubles. One episode can dramatically change your life and that of others. So, what can you do if you want to stay out of this stew?

Recent research suggests that explosive anger can co-occur with mood problems, anxiety, substance abuse, and posttraumatic stress disorder (Coccaro 2019). A national survey showed that people with emotional or substance abuse problems obtained some form of treatment about 60% of the time, while only 29% received professional treatment for anger (Kessler et al. 2006). Yet anger is a big deal, too! So, what are you to do?

Emotional labeling is one way to reduce these explosive anger episodes (Fahlgren et al. 2019). By pausing and naming the emotion you are feeling, you are off to a good start. However, what are your options if you are unsure, at first, about what you are feeling? One tip-off lies in what you are thinking. Here are some sample anger thinking themes: *I hate you. I'll hurt you. You shouldn't. You are to blame and are worthless.* You may not use the same words, but if the ideas are in that ballpark, label the feeling "anger." But what if you are aware of your anger but draw a blank on your thinking? Ask yourself, *If my anger were to speak with me, what would anger say?* Furthermore, what if a feeling of rage seems to come out of the blue? When this happens, pay attention to whether this feeling precedes or reflects a mood change. That information might be an early warning sign to take time out, to wait it out, or to act to change your mood.

For situations where you find that parasitic thinking fuses with explosive anger, what might you do to tone down anger thinking to buy yourself some time? Imagine your negative thinking as fluff on a down feather. Now, imagine the feather floating on a breeze over open space (a field of grass, a rolling river) with a blue sky overhead. Track the feather.

If you have a tendency toward intermittent explosive anger, you might have more empathy than the average person (Fahlgren et al. 2019). Below are some ways to turn that empathy inward to help you soften your reactions.

Think ahead. Write a message on a card that fits in your wallet or purse with this inscription: *If I were in the other person's shoes at this moment, how would I want others to treat me?* As you feel a rage escalating, take out the card and read it several times.

Switch the image. Instead of focusing your attention on the person you are targeting, imagine someone else in that person's place. Would you think the same negative things about your best friend, a favorite niece, or another person you care about who was doing the same thing?

This is an area where a combination of guided self-help and professional assistance can be helpful.

Top Tip: Stay Away from Dangerous Places

How often have you raised your voice, yelled, and hit someone, then later wished you had put your mind before your fist? Anonymous, who used his fists too often, spent his early twenties in prison. Then he learned to turn his life around. His journey from dangerous places began with a new idea, which serves as a helpful tip.

In the dangerous places in your mind, you want to hurt someone. You feel disrespected. You ask a stranger for directions, and the stranger walks away. You feel like yelling, "Hey man, don't you walk away from me!" Before you sink into the dangerous place, think about what is important and lasting. Is the situation more important and lasting than your family and friends? If you have a pet, who'd take care of your animal if something happened to you? How important is your freedom? Think about leaning on a tree watching a waterfall. How long do you want to be free to see it?

SHAME-ANGER PROBLEM SOLUTIONS

You've fallen short of your ideal standard. You exposed a shortcoming (as if you were the only one with shortcomings). You got drunk and vomited on the dinner table. When you feel conspicuous, with all eyes on you, that unpleasant feeling of shame reflects your self-view. Unlike guilt, which is an evaluation of negative actions, shame is a negative global feeling—an evaluation and condemnation of all of you. You feel the whole of you is disgraced and worthless when you view yourself as flawed before the eyes of all who behold you.

Shame is a trigger for anger and aggression (Tangney et al. 1996). Anger is the dark side to shame (Bear et al. 2009). If you tend to feel shame, you are more prone to anger and negative outcomes, particularly when shame is contaminated by a way of thinking referred to as *contingent worth*. We have a tangled web situation where shame and anger coexist. Shame represents worthlessness. Anger represents power. This is a logical inconsistency. However, we are psychological beings who are not necessarily classical logicians.

If you find yourself tangled in this web, here is an experiment for you.

You, like every other human being on this planet, are *pluralistic*. That means that you have hundreds of different attributes, including abilities, interests, values, emotions, traits, proclivities, habits, intellectual capabilities, and special qualities. You have uncountable experiences and learnings. You'll vary in your approach on a situational basis.

You are bound to have weak points and make errors. That's part of being human. You might even do more than your share of dumb things. You can surely judge and rate your actions. When it comes to giving yourself a global rating, you do so at your peril.

As all humans have more than their share of foibles and faults, to expect yourself to be a flawless exception is unrealistic. Accept that reality. You'll be less prone to fall into this contingent worth trap, where you base your worth on a flaw, a mistake, or an act of unfairness. This is like wearing a permanent scarlet letter, *W* (worthless), on the center of your forehead as a symbol of being ashamed forever. There has to be a better way.

Here is a question you can ask yourself if you feel ashamed and worthless: *If I am a pluralistic person, with many attributes and life experiences, how can I be only one thing,* worthless, *if I do something stupid?* The answer is that you can't be only one thing unless you accept a premise that you can only define yourself based on your screwups. On the other hand, by accepting your global self, while disliking some of your actions, you can get yourself out of a contingent worth trap and have less cause to anger yourself over your imperfections.

MY PROGRESS LOG

Key ideas: What three ideas did you pick up from this chapter that you found most helpful?

1.

2.

3.

Action plan: What three steps would you take to move closer to overcoming anger excesses?

1.

2.

3.

Execution: What are you going to do to execute the steps? (The process)

1.

2.

3.

Results: What do you hope to learn—or have reinforced—by taking these steps?

1.

2.

3.

Revisions: If you would make changes in the process, what would you do differently next time?

1.

2.

3.

CHAPTER 9

Assertive Solutions

Most people prefer to live their lives without infringing on the rights of others or having others trample on theirs. However, you also live in a social world where you'll have conflicts with others for one reason or another. People with values, beliefs, abilities, desires, and interests different from yours will be inclined to disagree with you, and some will try to take advantage of you. Some won't pay much attention to what they are doing and will figuratively step on your toes. How you handle yourself in these different circumstances makes a difference. Together, let's look at assertive options. We'll explore

- how assertiveness works from the vantage point of assertiveness masters,

- how to assess others' goals to judge how best to advocate for yourself,

- the importance of asserting yourself in complex situations where you face multiple conditions simultaneously, and

- extended benefits and downsides of an assertive philosophy.

PERSPECTIVES FROM ASSERTIVENESS MASTERS

If you don't advocate for yourself, who will? Sometimes a friend will help. Maybe you'll find a kindly stranger. However, advancing your enlightened self-interests is mostly up to you. Assertiveness is a process for self-advocacy where you act constructively to stand up for your rights and to advance your enlightened self-interests. An assertive philosophy differs radically from aggression, which is executing actions to cause harm. Assertiveness is about being in command of yourself and expressing yourself effectively with a positive impact.

People who tend to be very inhibited and people with harmful aggressive patterns approach learning assertion skills from different angles. Going from inhibition to assertiveness involves expanding authentic self-expressive capabilities. Going from aggression to assertiveness involves restricting aggressive behavior and expanding authentic self-expressive capabilities.

Assertiveness training began in the 1940s with therapist Andrew Salter's (1949) work on helping inhibited people to express their positive and negative emotions and dissatisfactions as well as to accept and express compliments. That original focus has expanded through the work of assertiveness pioneers Robert Alberti and Michael Emmons (2017).

Assertiveness is an often underutilized and yet very effective way to change negative factors that cut across different unpleasant conditions (Speed, Goldstein, and Goldfried 2018). For example, assertion is a leading substitute for aggression. By refining your assertiveness skills, you can express your feelings without the fallout from aggression.

Ten Assertiveness Strategies

The founder of logotherapy, psychiatrist Viktor Frankl, wrote that freedom is not a freedom from conditions, but rather the freedom to take a stand on whatever conditions confront you (1988). Between their first and their tenth edition of *Your Perfect Right*, Bob Alberti and Michael Emmons (1970, 2017) evolved their views to describe assertiveness as a form of self-expression for maintaining equal footing with other people in order to get along without trampling on them or letting them trample on you. Their approach includes reaching out to people, giving compliments, and apologizing when you are in the wrong.

The following chart describes ten methods of substituting assertion for aggression, along with their purposes. Keep in mind that context is important; withholding assertions is appropriate when speaking up would produce greater harm. When considering an assertive response to a problem, you might want to refer to this chart to help identify your purpose and decide on an approach.

Assertiveness Strategy	Purpose
Act in a timely way.	Address or resolve a conflict sooner to avoid festering and accelerating anger.
Take responsibility for what you are thinking and saying.	Say what you want unambiguously and avoid unnecessary confusion.
Defuse extension-of-blame thinking.	Increase receptivity to reduce defensiveness and save time going through the weeds of that quagmire.
Give and take compliments comfortably.	Complimenting others and accepting compliments aids positive relationships and reduces anger within such relationships.
Decide when a hassle isn't worth the hassle.	You can challenge just about everything you don't like. Putting the time into doing what you do like may be more important to do.
Maintain normal eye contact.	Demonstrate confidence and conviction with eye contact without trying to stare someone down or looking askance.

Keep a comfortable distance.	Avoid intruding into someone's space and evoking a territorial anger reaction (about three feet in the US is usually a comfortable distance).
Project a comfortable posture.	When you feel relaxed, this signals a comfortable, confident, capable way of being.
Accept criticism and feedback realistically.	Helpful feedback and criticism invite an approving response, such as "Thanks for sharing that with me. I appreciate that."
Identify a point of common ground.	When you have legitimate points of disagreement, start an exchange in an area where you have more "give and take."

A Twelve-Step Assertiveness Approach

Advancing your enlightened self-interests involves building bridges between yourself and others. The following twelve assertiveness steps can get you onto that bridge.

Take the situation seriously but not personally. When you focus on what you want to accomplish, and not on your ego, your thought processes are more likely to flow fluidly. You may see problems before you feel their results.

Maintain a nonjudgmental attitude. When you separate people from their behavior, you can accept the person but not the unacceptable behavior. At first, most need to make a deliberate effort to make that separation. When people feel accepted, they are more likely to look at their positions critically. Meanwhile, an assertive position is not an inflexible one but rather molded by facts as they evolve.

Work out your anger first. You are likely to assert yourself effectively when your mind is largely free of parasitic anger thoughts. Here are some quick-check issues: Have I diminished my extension-of-blame thinking? Have I freed myself from overgeneralization? Have I avoided a fundamental attribution error? (See chapter 2 for a refresher on attribution errors.) Have I accepted the situation for what it is?

Come down on the right side of an issue. In some situations, you'll have value choices. Here is a simple technique to gain clarity on such choices. Ask yourself these questions: *If I were to do this, what would I gain? What would I lose? Who would this action hurt, and why? In an ambiguous situation, would I wisely get independent information before acting?* "Thinking about it" is an assertive action.

Think beyond the moment. Sighting beyond the moment can help maintain perspective. The following questions can help: *What do I want to accomplish? What types of relationships do I prefer to build?* By thinking beyond the moment, you can avoid an anger impulse that can sabotage the positive outcomes you want.

Check your tone for naturalness. Set the tone, and you set the direction. When you express yourself in a natural, nonhostile, open, agreeable manner, you are more likely to have a favorable impact. An open, natural tone increases your chances of hearing the same tone in response.

Be mindful of the language you use. Pejorative terms can inflame others. Use them, and you may trigger a tit-for-tat situation where one negative word begets another. You are more likely to assert your position effectively without using language to put others on the defensive. Communications are a two-way street. If the other guy uses pejorative words, what's your option? You can join the fray, or you can model accurate but nonpejorative language. You can confront the issue and point out how put-downs, belittling, or other emotionally charged words are conversation stoppers, and then take it from there.

Speak from the concept. The concept is the idea behind your words. In a spontaneous conversation, if you try to think out every word, you can distract yourself from changing conditions and put yourself into a vulnerable position. *Speaking from the concept* means that you are clear on the issue and the idea that you want to get across. Your words will reflect that clarity.

Express facts objectively. Gather facts (beforehand by research or in the process by questioning). Use the best information available. Emphasize what you have the greatest confidence in saying. Especially check other's views in ambiguous situations. Clarify misunderstandings with verifiable information.

Stick with the issues. Because communications are a two-way street between people who may have different views, keeping on track and on target while others have their say, too, is the ideal behind assertive communications. You can choose what you say and do. You can exercise that choice to focus your attention on matters of importance.

Make your three major points. It often happens that you miss saying something and, in hindsight, wish that you said what you later thought to say. That's common. To reduce this risk, think about your three main points and get them out early.

Escalate when necessary. Start with the minimal assertion to help you achieve the results you seek. Add points and clarity on where you stand. In considering this escalation method, balance others' feelings and probable interpretations against the benefits you may gain. This saying applies: *To crack an eggshell, you don't need a sledgehammer.*

Now it's time for you to put these steps to use in the following experiment.

MY TWELVE-STEP ASSERTIVENESS PROGRAM

When you act assertively, do you experience a greater sense of freedom? That's the experiment. In the following chart, the first column lists the twelve steps we discussed above. When you know you have an upcoming conflict, such as disputing a bill or resolving a difference in views about an issue, review the steps in column one. At the conclusion of the conflict, fill in the second column with the actions you took in the conflict situation, then list the results in the third column.

Assertiveness Step	What I Did	What Resulted
Take the situation seriously but not personally.		
Maintain a nonjudgmental attitude.		
Work out your anger first.		
Come down on the right side of an issue.		
Think beyond the moment.		
Check your tone for naturalness.		
Be mindful of the language you use.		
Speak from the concept.		
Express facts objectively.		
Stick with the issues.		
Make your three major points.		
Escalate when necessary.		

By repeating the process many times, you practice developing your assertive skills and effectively resolving conflicts in your enlightened self-interests. You are free to change your mind if you discover the facts don't warrant escalating assertive actions or the costs significantly exceed the benefits.

THE GOAL TECHNIQUE

You must be living on top of an isolated mountain if you don't occasionally find people who are *too into themselves* to pay attention to the world around them, or *out for themselves* and don't care much whether they inconvenience you or others. These situations present special assertiveness challenges.

Here is a too rarely asked question that makes sense to routinely ask yourself: *What's the person's goal?* The question serves as a temporary distancing technique for pausing and avoiding jumping to conclusions and overreacting. But it is so much more. By hypothesizing about another's goal in a situation, you can assess how much flexibility you'll have in negotiating solutions to a mutual problem, when you are likely to meet an impasse, and whether you have a broad or restricted range of options. Hypotheses, however, are beliefs that need to be tested. Nevertheless, keep that hypothesized goal in mind and you might reduce a tendency to extend blame and to lose sight of your own goals.

The goal technique applies to most situations involving assertiveness. Here is an adverse event example: You are waiting in line at the supermarket. An elderly woman fumbles for coupons in her overly filled purse while arguing with the cashier about accepting an expired one. What's her goal? You can reasonably assume she wants to save money. As a background issue, you suspect that she could use help getting organized. You might conclude that she is out to get a dollar benefit (goal) and is too absorbed to pay much attention to what is happening around her (background). Would you be inclined to insert yourself into the situation and assert an interest for her to move along? If you are feeling peeved, would your goal be to let off steam? Would your goal be to hurry her up? Would your goal be to "let it go" because getting into a feud could cause you a further delay?

When people inconvenience you because they are not paying attention to what they are doing, most stop when you matter-of-factly call this to their attention. Their implicit goal is likely to work something out in their head, and some lose sight of what is going on around them. Some assertion situations have complications that normally take longer to resolve. For example, your normally reclusive neighbor starts installing a corrugated steel garden shed with a corner two feet on your property. In a matter-of-fact way, you approach the neighbor and point to your property pin and kindly volunteer to help move the shed over. Your neighbor tells you, "You must have moved the pin. Why are you making a big deal out of this? It's a woody area. No one uses it anyway." The neighbor turns away and keeps working on the shed.

What's the neighbor's goal? The obvious one is to leave the shed where it is. The neighbor may have an additional goal to avoid the hassle of moving the shed. What's your goal? If it is to get the shed off your property, here is a sample assertion: in a naturally clear, confident, and determined tone, you inform the neighbor that unless he can prove you moved the pin, he needs to move the shed onto his property before the end of the day. Communicating a time line can create pressure. You are now free to walk away. (I've personally found that a clear, confident, time-based action can be effective, but not all the time.)

An assertive escalation approach often starts with a simple declarative statement about what you want in the context of recognizing another's goals. The idea is to do just enough to bring about the results that you seek, and if the first step isn't sufficient, you step it up a level. Let's say the neighbor didn't move the shed. You might hire a surveyor to confirm your property line. (It's normally useful to work off facts, and this is one of those instances.) Validating the pin location might be the push you need to cause the neighbor to move the shed. You present the facts. This neighbor won't budge. You have another step to take.

You've validated the location of the pin. You present your case to law enforcement and ask for help, and that should end the issue. However, if your neighbor still won't budge (some have an irrational drive to prove they can do as they choose), you can escalate to a legal solution and force the neighbor to move the shed. Whatever the outcome, plan for an angry neighbor.

COMPLEX ASSERTIVENESS SITUATIONS

In some conflict situations, many can benefit from your assertive actions. For example, at the last minute, the airline canceled your flight while you were waiting at the gate. The plane was to make a few stops, so passengers needing to make connecting flights would likely miss the connection. Thirty or more people lined up to reschedule their flights.

The first passenger at the counter yells at the representative that he has a critical meeting to attend. He demands a private plane. The passenger is on a rant, and this goes on for over seven minutes with no end in sight. The flustered clerk apologizes while telling him he'd have to schedule a later flight or go with another airline. The goal of the ranting passenger is getting a flight out as soon as possible, perhaps to discharge tension over the inconvenience. The agent's goal is to get the passenger off her back and get to work with the others. The goal of the other thirty people, including the second passenger in line, Jed, is to get service quickly and arrange for other flights.

In a matter-of-fact tone, Jed said, "Excuse me, sir. I'm with you, buddy, rotten break. But look behind you. There is a long line of people steamed up about waiting. If you don't mind my suggestion, what about taking this to a supervisor who has the authority to make things happen?" The first passenger nodded yes.

Looking at the clerk, Jed asked, "Can you get a supervisor for this gentleman? He has an important meeting and needs a resolution." The agent made the call. Passenger one was, in this instance, happy to have support. He walked to the area where he'd meet the supervisor. Jed said to the clerk, "It looks like you are going to have a rough morning. Sorry about that." The clerk went out of her way to find Jed a flight.

Could you have rehearsed responding to this and every other situation? I doubt it. Will every situation of this sort work out as you wish? Probably not. Sure, you'll encounter people who won't budge from their agenda because (1) their goal is to stand their ground, (2) they have too much ego at stake to be accommodating, (3) they lack flexibility, or (4) they believe they are entitled to do as they wish. Sometimes the trade-off in time and effort isn't worth the gain to use an assertion approach. You can't win them all.

Get enough practice in asserting your interest in achieving your goal, while being mindful of what others want to accomplish, and at some point, you may find that much of what you've practiced comes together to where assertion feels natural.

CREATING AN ASSERTIVE PHILOSOPHY

There is more to assertiveness than sending overcooked meals back at a restaurant or saying something to the person in front of you in line who is telling their life story to a bored cashier. Assertiveness applies to situations where you pursue a love interest, take steps to get an education, create a desirable career, and more. The idea, as expressed earlier, is to go after what you want without needlessly harming others.

You can approach assertiveness as a practical life philosophy for situations where advocating for and advancing your interests is important to do. However, an assertive philosophy does not come naturally for many. Indeed, evolving this philosophy takes practicing basic assertiveness skills and applying them to longer-term problem-solving challenges.

Might assertiveness have its downsides? Having an expert assertive style does not guarantee you will get your point across, resolve a problem, or prevent an ongoing contentious situation. You may not win many popularity contests when you advocate for yourself and clash with another's interests. Although you might be influential, you can't control another's perspective and reaction. Here is a sample of downsides to assertiveness:

- Some situations involve negotiations and tradeoffs. You are disadvantaged by another's actions. The other is willing to make an adjustment but not to completely acquiesce and therefore won't budge. Sometimes you won't get 100% of what you want without incurring other costs. Taking less than what you want to resolve a problem is a choice, too.

- In situations where someone is acting intentionally unfairly and you skillfully and nonjudgmentally respond with a fact-based assertion, you'll most likely get a defensive reaction, even if you were the poster person of the year on assertiveness. In general, people who engage in exploitative activities don't want anyone to call them out.

- When you present your positions in a clear, positive, reasonable, and confident way, some might still seek to advantage themselves. There is extensive scientific literature demonstrating that many people will overestimate their capabilities.

- You might overwhelm some who lack confidence in themselves, leading to brooding resentment and later actions to undermine you. However, you might reduce your risk for this type of outcome by operating fairly while being mindful of areas of mutual interest.

Although most people won't like being the target of an assertion, they probably would prefer that to an angry-aggressive approach. Anticipating some ill will is sometimes the price of protecting your interests. In the next chapter you'll learn about an active-reflective form of communication that can soften an assertion and increase your effectiveness.

MY PROGRESS LOG

Key ideas: What three ideas did you pick up from this chapter that you found most helpful?

1.

2.

3.

Action plan: What three steps would you take to move closer to overcoming anger excesses?

1.

2.

3.

Execution: What are you going to do to execute the steps? (The process)

1.

2.

3.

Results: What do you hope to learn—or have reinforced—by taking these steps?

1.

2.

3.

Revisions: If you would make changes in the process, what would you do differently next time?

1.

2.

3.

CHAPTER 10

How to Communicate Effectively with Impact

While in a stress-anger-stress cycle (chapter 6), you'll probably find yourself muddling some of your communications and possibly later regretting some things that you said or didn't say. Can you prevent, or break, the cycle with active-reflective communications? Together we'll explore assertive communication strategies that can boost your communication skills in potentially contentious situations. Specifically, we'll look at how to

- weed out false anger assumptions and improve your communications with yourself,

- make a productive impact through active-reflective communications,

- use assertive questioning and set the agenda to prevent someone from catching you off guard, and

- take charge of your agenda.

ASSUMPTION CHECKING

There is little research on the connection between assumptions and anger. Yet assumptions blend with parasitic forms of anger as ink in water. So, let's isolate anger-driving assumptions and explore how to break free from this hidden burden.

We make assumptions all the time. Assumptions are what you accept as true without proof or take for granted as settled facts. Like beliefs, some assumptions prove accurate, some contain partial truths, and some have as much value as a single grain of sand. Until recognized as contestable, they are beyond contesting. Assumptions range from almost certain to self-deceptive fictions. Here is a sample of both kinds of assumptions.

- If you drop an apple from a tree, it will fall. How many times have you seen an apple start dropping from a tree and turn and head toward the stratosphere? The law of gravity explains the fall.

- It's almost certain that when you turn on your kitchen water faucet, water will flow. You've made a good assumption. You have no guarantee you will be right 100% of the time, but who would bet against you?

- You may have heard that people use only 10% of their brains. The idea is that genius is within your reach with a bit more of your brain power. Meanwhile, what is the other 90% doing, loafing? There is no compelling evidence to support that assumption.

- Extensions of blame fuse with faulty assumptions, such as if someone displeases you, they are rotten to the core and deserve the worst. The assumption is that you should have authority to cause harm and pain. Where's the proof of that?

- On the self-deceptive end of the assumption scale, you assume events make you angry. Your train is late, and you feel angry. You act as if you assume you have no choice but to feel this way. An acquaintance turns away from you. Does this force you to feel angry? What if you jumped to this conclusion before you saw that the person was fainting?

False assumptions are behind many misperceptions. If you jump to a conclusion about someone's intentions, and anger yourself, what's the proof of the assumption about their intentions? If you have a strong negative bias against a political figure, are your assumptions the same as that of the candidate's closest supporters and friends? Who's right?

Assumption checking begins with an awareness of the critical assumptions that you think are true in each conflict situation. Figuring that out isn't as tough as it may seem. The next time you feel anger, ask yourself, *What am I assuming in this situation?* Let's say your response is, *I have no choice but to feel angry if I don't like what someone does.* Does that assumption extend to your best friend? If not, you found an exception to the assumption and possible freedom from the fallacy.

Some assumptions link together into a compound. Let's explore four potential assumptions in an extension-of-blame pattern: (1) the person instigated the problem, (2) the deed was done on purpose, (3) the person should not have done this, and (4) you are justified in doing whatever you want to cause harm. Let's do a validity check on the third part of this compound process. This assumption boils down to *the event should not have happened*. Demanding that something that happened shouldn't have happened is a *counterfactual assertion*, or something that is not factual. A counterfactual assertion is as solid as assuming that Tinker Bell is real. If you recognize that demandingness is more the issue and based on dubious assumptions, you've taken a strong step to break the linchpin in a chain of extension-of-blame assumptions.

If you're not sure if an assumption that you regularly apply is false or not, you can often tell by its results. If you anger yourself too often and too intensely, ask yourself, *What am I assuming? Where is the evidence for the assumption? Will the assumption stand up in court as fact?*

Here is a brief awareness exercise for recognizing assumptions and for doing a validity check. Use a recent (or upcoming) situation for a reference.

Situation: _____

Questions on Assumptions	Answers on Assumptions
What are my assumptions about this situation?	
What evidence supports the assumption(s)?	
If a skilled lawyer cross-examined me, would this evidence hold up in court?	

By eliminating false or marginal assumptions, you've helped yourself lessen stress and anger fused to those assumptions.

ACTIVE-REFLECTIVE COMMUNICATIONS

Others have assumptions, too. They will sometimes (maybe often) veer from yours. How many angry arguments stem from differences in assumptions? Probably quite a few. After you've checked your assumptions, checking another's assumptions is an assertive way to nip a problem in the bud and resolve differences while getting across the points you want to make. How might you do this without being intrusive and setting off another problem? The process of active-reflective communication can help you refine your assertive-expressive skills.

Active-reflective communicating is a process for

- building bridges when warranted and strengthening the bridges that you have when you find structural problems;

- expressing yourself and hearing others out on occasions when it is important to be mindful of others' views;

- gathering information to decide where you can make accommodations, when you'd wisely hold your ground, and when you've hit a stone wall; and

■ finding a workable resolution based on a joint understanding of the issues.

An active-reflective communicating process involves pausing, reflecting, gathering information, reasoning based on that information, and employing that information to solve a problem. This approach can help reduce or end the emotional intensity of negative interactions.

Guidelines for Active-Reflective Communicating

Communications intended to confront unpleasant situations or to resolve conflicts rarely follow a straight line. I think of active-reflective communicating more as an art with some common sense and science blended in. The process is like selecting paint from a palette of different colors and using the paintbrush creatively. You may have to paint over a color. Perhaps a wavy line will project better than a straight one will.

Active-reflective communications are also like tools in a toolbox; each has a different function. Some do the same thing but in different ways. You decide what you'll practice using. You control the use of these tools and which ones fit the situation. With practice, this becomes a natural way of thinking and communicating.

Between the paint and the tools you have ingredients to communicate effectively with impact. The following are suggestions of how to approach situations using active-reflective communication and some conditions to avoid:

■ Avoid making negative first impressions. Skeptical tones, negative body language, and extension-of-blame messages are often provocative, gin up resistance, and dampen your chances for a resolution.

■ Focus on what the speaker says. Hold back on inserting your thoughts into the subject until you understand the issue from the other's perspective (most skip this important step). Although you may disagree with the other person, it is normally useful to know what they are thinking.

■ Avoid prematurely taking center stage to get out the message you want heard. Blend your message into the conversation in a give-and-take way that fits naturally. When you prematurely present information, you might come across as a classroom lecturer who can't wait to get your message out. Your message can get lost that way.

■ Avoid the common tendency to make statements in a contentious situation or to ask questions that are demand statements in disguise, such as, "Why do you act that way?" (Translation: you should not act that way; act as I expect you to.) That's a discussion stopper.

■ Ask questions to gather the information that can broaden your perspective and the perspective of the other; you are likely to learn more this way. For example, you might ask, "What do you see as the problem?" "What might we do to turn this around that works for both of us?" "What do you think about doing _____?"

■ Rephrase for clarity. When in doubt about the meaning of another's perspective, seek clarity: "It sounds like you are saying…" "Is this what you mean…?" "Correct me if I'm wrong, but this is my understanding of your position…" (The other person, upon hearing an "instant replay," can clear up inaccuracies or misconceptions.) You'll verify or disconfirm some of your assumptions. If you erred, you'll find out.

■ Advice from the eighteenth-century American inventor, publisher, and diplomat Ben Franklin, still holds: take ownership of your views. Begin statements with phrases such as "I believe," "It seems to me," or "It appears to me." By expressing yourself with "I feel" or "I believe" assertions, you are less likely to put someone on the defensive.

■ Pay close attention not only to the words others use, but also to their tone, facial expression, and posture. (Pupils may dilate when you experience something interesting and contract in anger-triggering situations.) What you see signals the emotions behind the words.

■ Body language—along with word choice, tone, and inflection—is part of the message. Thus, pay attention to your tone, your body language, and the words you use. What is your body language saying? Does your body language fit with your verbal messages?

■ Maintain perspective on socially acceptable anger expressions. Depending on the circumstances, a genuine expression of indignation can have a positive impact. Politicians who express themselves in angry tones may appear unpleasant and out of control. Know your audience!

■ Be authentic. Both observation and psychological research suggest that authenticity in purpose and tone conveys a direct message. A genuine and warranted angry tone gets attention, focuses attention, and can prove impactful in situations where anger is appropriate (Shuman, Halperin, and Reifen Tagar 2018), providing you are not pushing to change someone's values (Harinck and Van Kleef 2012).

■ Listen to ego cues. These are ways people have of spinning situations to maintain an image or to deflect from an issue, often making you, others, or situations the subject of blame. The absence or presence of this information is useful to assess a situation.

■ Refrain from using accusatory language. Most people tune in to negatives. It's a survival thing that probably started with the first protozoa that survived by moving from the source of a negative sensation. An accusatory "you" ("You did this") is likely to evoke a negative feeling and invite a defensive response. Although the issue is more the intent and the tone than the word "you" itself, in conflict situations, why risk a misunderstanding?

■ Avoid blame-labeling (chapter 4), such as saying, "It's your fault and you're a blankety-blank piece of crap for doing that." Most people understandably get their hackles up and respond negatively to communications when they are blame-labeled. You probably would, too. You might be right on the issue, but this will move you further from a potential resolution.

■ Keep your assertions positive and just enough to influence a change ("just enough" is difficult to assess at times) to improve your chances for cooperation. You can overwhelm some people with assertive communication, making cooperation that much more difficult.

- Demonstrate a confident but respectful attitude. With this approach, an equitable exchange will be more likely and others will be more likely to reciprocate.

- Separate the person from their performance. People are pluralistic, not caricatures of a negative label. Most problems boil down to perceived or real negative actions that people take. Focus on behavioral changes that are relevant and mutually beneficial.

By improving your expressive and assertiveness skills and by treating others fairly, you boost your odds that you'll enjoy more cooperative relationships.

Changing Through Contemplation

A martial artist hones many skills. Developing these skills takes hundreds of hours of practice. Likewise, active-reflective communication skills take mental preparation and practice in simulations and real-time incidents until they feel natural. Let's start with a contemplation experiment as a tool to build communication skills.

MY CONTEMPLATION EXPERIMENT

By contemplating using specific active-reflective communication methods, you are preparing to express yourself more effectively. Take five minutes each day to contemplate the meaning of ten assertive communication strategies featured in chapter 9 and this chapter. Do this experiment for five minutes a day for ten days. On each day, contemplate using one of the assertiveness strategies in the left column in an imagined or real situation. For example, on day one, imagine what you would look like, say, and do to create a positive first impression and to avoid making a negative one. Day five is the eye-contact experiment. Imagine yourself comfortably maintaining eye contact without staring, glaring, or glancing away. Possibly create a pleasant fantasy conversation with someone while you maintain eye contact.

At the end of each five-minute session, record what you learned from each contemplation experiment.

Assertiveness Strategy	What I Learned from the Contemplation
Present a positive first impression and avoid making a negative one.	
Take responsibility for what you are thinking and saying.	

Refuse to engage in extension-of-blame thinking.	
Decide when a hassle isn't worth the hassle and do something else instead.	
Maintain eye contact.	
Keep a comfortable distance.	
Project a comfortable posture.	
Avoid accusatory "you" statements.	
Rephrase for clarity.	
Accept criticism and feedback realistically.	

This form of guided contemplation is a step in the direction of substituting assertion for aggression by considering assertive alternatives. Experiment with different amounts of time and different assertive ideas. See if this practice carries over to action situations.

USING ASSERTIVE QUESTIONING

From time to time, someone catches you off guard, asks you to do a favor, and you feel as if you are in a corner. As an afterthought, someone coined the phrase "I should have seen this coming." However, all the *could haves* and *should haves* don't change what was.

It is easier to say yes than no. It's like someone paying you in advance for a future effort. Sometimes it is important to know what "yes" will entail. Assertive questions help. Let's look at an example. Jasper called you to help with a house project. He asked you to come over and give him a hand installing a toilet. You know he lives about forty minutes from you. You don't know Jasper that well. It's reasonable to find out what he has in mind.

You: Okay. Walk me through the paces. Exactly what would I be doing, and how long would it take?

Jasper: It's no big deal. It will take just a little while.

You: It's an eighty-minute drive back and forth for me. How about a nearby neighbor?

Jasper: They are busy.

You: Okay, what would you need me to do?

Jasper: We'd have to reroute some of the water lines for the sink.

You: What has that got to do with the toilet?

Jasper: I'm redoing the bathroom.

You: What else do you have in mind for me to do?

Jasper: You have good mechanical skills. I thought you'd be a good person to help me out.

You: Thanks for the invitation. I'll pass on that.

The important thing is deciding what is in your interests to do and having the information to make an informed decision. By getting enough information, you put yourself in a position to make that decision. You've spared yourself a needless hassle and possibly some resentment.

When in doubt, here is an assertive alternative: "I'll think about it."

Top Tip: Expressing Anger Assertively Is Expressing Anger Effectively

You and your mate agree on a change to make your relationship better. You uphold the bargain. Your mate doesn't. If you stuff healthy anger to appease your mate, both of you are likely to suffer. Ridgewood, New Jersey, psychologist Dr. Jeff Rudolph tackles this suppressed anger problem by showing how to assert yourself effectively with your mate.

Here's a practical *escalation ladder plan* to prevent anger suppression and improve your communications. On the first step of this ladder, ask your mate to help you get into the practice of asserting your preferences. Start with a topic where you both disagree on some points, but not all (e.g., politics, private versus public education). In turn, you and your mate listen without comment. The time frame is two minutes each. Do this once a day for three days. At the next step on the ladder, you and your partner create an emotional safe zone to listen and learn from each other about where you'd like to see changes. The rules are simple. You each take two minutes to express what you want. You don't interrupt, blame, negate, or later retaliate. The next day, see if you can work out a give-and-take deal on the change where you each play a specific part. The next step is for more intimate communications. You move to a *debate to relate* level, where you express yourselves humanely and assertively on matters that are positive as well as negative: feelings of warmth, empathy, concerns, and anger-related issues. With meaningful, intimate exchanges, you are likely to have less anger to express and none to suppress.

SETTING THE AGENDA

Most agendas are normal. You are in negotiations to buy a landscape painting at a tag sale for your "scenes for serenity" project. You don't like the price. You know how much you are willing to pay. How you'll accomplish buying the painting at or below the price you want to pay is part of your agenda.

Most people intuitively know the difference between a negotiation agenda, an agenda for a meeting, and a hidden agenda driven by aggressive, ulterior motives. Nefarious, hidden agenda situations are relatively rare but highly memorable. The problem is that such hidden agendas are not obvious.

You may not have many opportunities to practice debunking and avoiding hidden agendas that affect you. Because of the spacing in time between encountering harmful agendas, and the differences in the agendas, another adage, "Once burned, twice shy," rarely applies. So how do you get to practice?

In developing your hidden-agenda recognition skills, observe political talk show hosts. Ask yourself, *What's the agenda?* You'll often find hosts who act as if their opinions are facts. There will be omissions, of course. Look for what is missing, which is the other side of the story. What's missing is often significant. What's embellished? Do you detect snide put-downs of others' positions?

Here are two questions that can guide your thinking about any agenda: *If I bought into this agenda, where would this lead?* and *If I looked for exceptions to the message, would the picture change?* Your answers to these questions can lead to clarity about the agenda.

Controlling the Agenda

Whoever controls the agenda shapes the outcome. Take charge of yourself in this area, and you are likely to have fewer regrets and incidents of reactive anger that can come about when you lose control over a situation. When you hold the high cards, you have a right to play them. Let's look at a major issue, a home purchase, where the high-card principle applies and someone wants to take that control from you.

You have a criterion for the kind of home you want. A home purchase is a big investment. You don't do this every day, so those who do this for a living can assert an advantage. They've got the norms for how to negotiate deals using other people's money.

You contacted a real estate agent a friend recommended. Your agent wants to control the agenda and make a quick sale. She wants to narrow your choices quickly, point out the benefits for each property, and try to get you to pick one. She pushes for an answer. She argues that if you don't buy now, someone else will scoop up the properties. You are prepared to walk away from a hurried deal. You remain in the driver's seat if you are willing to hold on to the wheel.

You hold the high cards. You have the credit. You have the down payment. Knowing where you stand, and where you control the agenda, simplifies dealing with agenda-driven people who can only control an agenda when you relinquish your authority.

Sadly, you can't prepare for all possible agendas. Too many exist. You can, however, take what you learn from each situation and apply this to the next potential anger-evoking situation. Here's a thought from the originator of assertiveness: "Never play another person's game. Play your own" (Salter 1949, 51).

For more information on assertive practices and expressions, check out Alberti and Emmons's (2017) book *Your Perfect Right*.

MY PROGRESS LOG

Key ideas: What three ideas did you pick up from this chapter that you found most helpful?

1.

2.

3.

Action plan: What three steps would you take to move closer to overcoming anger excesses?

1.

2.

3.

Execution: What are you going to do to execute the steps? (The process)

1.

2.

3.

Results: What do you hope to learn—or have reinforced—by taking these steps?

1.

2.

3.

Revisions: If you would make changes in the process, what would you do differently next time?

1.

2.

3.

CHAPTER 11

Mastery over Anger

Along with practically everyone else, your efforts to overcome parasitic anger and aggression will follow an irregular path. Let's see how to smooth out the process. Together, we'll look at

- resolving conflicts between primal emotional reactions and reasoning,

- five stages of change for strengthening your abilities to overcome parasitic anger, and

- how freedom involves responsible restrictions.

You can apply this three-phase change plan to practically any situation that involves a meaningful, personal change.

CONFLICTS BETWEEN IMPULSE AND REASON

Various experts have developed theories and approaches regarding the different processes that affect how we respond to situations, including conflicts. Sigmund Freud, the founder of psychoanalysis, used a horse-and-rider metaphor to describe the struggle between impulse and reason. The horse represents primal ways of doing and learning. As a creature of instincts, habits, and patterns, when the horse has an urge to graze, it grazes. It approaches what feels pleasant and avoids what does not. The horse runs with its herd, rests when it chooses, and mates when it can. The rider, who represents reason, does what the horse can't. No horse wrote a best-selling book or designed a bridge. Relative to the rider, the horse is a slow learner. Nevertheless, it operates with powerful emotional tools that can influence rider choices.

Let's take a closer look at some theories that emerged from this concept.

The Dual Process

The horse-and-rider metaphor was one of many early run-ups to *dual process theory*, which holds that two main processes influence how you respond to situations. The first is automatic, where perceptions stimulate primal brain regions. Emotions, impulses, surviving, thriving, seeking pleasure, and avoiding pain are part of this process. To neuroscientist and psychologist Antonio Damasio (2017), emotions and "feelings tell the mind, without any word being spoken, of the good and bad life process…" (p. 12).

The second process is slower, deliberate, and engages memories, reason, language, knowledge, and other cognitive processes. Based on the first process, you might make an impulse purchase of a TV because of an urge. But your cognitive brain takes a different path. You slow down and research TVs to find what model is most reliable and best for your use.

System 1 and System 2 Thinking

Nobel prize winner and psychologist Daniel Kahneman's (2011) *System 1 and System 2* metaphor describes a popular view of how your brain processes information. System 1 is unconscious, automatic, and wired to emotions, such as anger and fear. System 1 relies on intuition, heuristics (rules of thumb, trial and error), and doing things fast by rote. If I ask what is 2 + 2, you don't have to think it out. Your answer comes fast. System 1 is also a primary reservoir for parasitic anger thinking honed from years of practice. Unchecked biases, distortions, and irrational anger cognitions reside in that reservoir, along with intuitively accurate views. The problem is telling one from the other in provocative situations.

If you need to calculate 132 x 45 – 16 ÷ 3, this is a System 2 process. System 2 is deliberate, analytical, and effortful; it requires more resources. It takes a System 2 effort to defuse reactive forms of parasitic anger.

By practicing countermeasures to System 1 parasitic anger reactions, System 2 thinking, feeling, and behaving can become semiautomatic. Let's look at how you might turn a deliberate process into a positive, fast-thinking habit of reducing needless anger.

The *Y* Choice

You come to a fork in the road where you can choose to go an automatic, parasitic anger way or combat a defective anger process. You have a "*Y* choice." The *Y* symbolizes the fork in the road. Here is what you face at this fork in the road. The horse, emotional impulse, and System 1 pull in one direction. The rider, reason (including foresight), and System 2 face a double challenge: (1) resisting an automatic impulse to veer onto the path of parasitic anger, and (2) taking steps to distance yourself, reflecting, reasoning, separating fiction from fact, generating perspective, and judging what's in your enlightened self-interest to do. When you recognize the choice, you have an advantage.

If you choose to follow the problem-solving path, how do you take advantage of what you know about the horse and rider, dual process, and Systems 1 and 2 thinking? Let's consider three factors that work in your favor:

- You feel the effects of a parasitic anger belief but find it challenging to let go of the belief that external events are the sole cause of anger. You might ask yourself, *If anger spoke to me, what sentences would I find in the shadows of my mind?* You see your part in this process. That can get you to the next level of awareness and a *Y* choice.

- You recognize the parasitic belief(s) that links with excess anger. You've come to another pivotal point. You can choose to challenge the anger belief or choose to give the horse the reins. You might ask yourself, *What do I gain or lose on each branch of the path?* Asking that question is another victory over unrestrained impulse.

- In this instance, you chose to act against parasitic beliefs. You accept that you'll need to make a deliberate effort and probably multiple ones. You reach into your psychological toolkit for what you think applies to the situation.

It takes work beyond choosing to change from an automated to an effortful and intensive cognitive path. It is what it is. You have a problem to solve. You can either duck or do it.

Automating System 2 Thinking

Can you turn deliberate, purposeful, and effortful coping techniques into semiautomatic processes? It depends on the techniques. Here are a few:

- Turning *Y* choice recognition into a routine response in anger-provoking situations

- Using practical techniques, like deep breathing or taking a walk

- Practicing cognitive reappraisal techniques to improve your future initial appraisals

The following coping statement approach is another candidate for conversion to a semiautomatic process.

Priming Your Coping Statements

Priming refers to doing something to stimulate something. You may prime your lawnmower with gas so that it will start. You can prime yourself to approach anger-triggering situations you want to handle nonparasitically using coping statements.

Coping statements are true, believable substitutions for fictional parasitic self-talk. For example, in a parasitic mindset, when you are not getting what you want, you might tell yourself the equivalent of *I can't stand not having my way. I'll fix that lousy SOB.* In contrast, here is a priming coping statement for preparing yourself to respond assertively: *I prefer getting what I want. It's not the end of the world if I don't.*

Coping statement lists are often like a smorgasbord of statements, such as "I'll live through it." Let's look at an alternative approach that uses clusters of coping statement sequences to go a step further. Here, you prime your thoughts with logically ordered coping statements, such as, *I'll check the ideas behind my anger impulses by checking my facts.*

A cluster of priming coping statements has at least these potential benefits: (1) helping you gain distance from a situation, (2) serving as a substitute for System 1 parasitic thinking, and (3) guiding you toward a constructive action. When practiced, the cluster sequence can evolve into a semiautomatic process.

The following chart is an experiment using two sample clusters of coping statement sequences. Column one shows sample coping statements. Column two is the activating situation. In column three, you record the results of this experiment. Review the coping sequence now, then use it as a resource for a future situation. When you test the coping sequence, record what you do and what resulted. This gives you some ideas for adjustments.

Coping Sequence	Situation	Results
1. I can recognize anger-triggering events. 2. I can pause and do a quick breathing exercise. 3. I can advance my interests assertively.		
1. The situation is what it is. 2. If I feel uncomfortable, so be it. 3. I can handle myself effectively, even if imperfectly. 4. I don't have to take parasitic thoughts seriously.		

Unless you needlessly anger yourself multiple times each day and have plenty of occasions to practice, you may need to create opportunities to automate a coping statement cluster system. Below is a visualization experiment that you can do daily or until your coping statements come to mind quickly by rote.

In column one of the following chart, list ten mild parasitic anger situations, such as "My toast was in the toaster too long." In column two, input a cluster of coping statements. (The same cluster might cover all ten situations, or you might have more than one cluster you want to test.) Create your own sequence or use one of my examples from above.

Here is the experiment. After you've filled in the table, imagine the first situation. With the image in mind, rehearse the coping statement sequence in your mind four times. If the cluster of coping statements seems helpful, continue to the next situation. If not, modify the statement(s).

Parasitic Anger Trigger	Coping Statement Cluster

If coping statements are not your cup of tea, you can shift gears and imagine each provocative situation as a puff of steam disappearing into the air. That can lessen the intensity of your emotive cognitions (thoughts with the power to evoke emotions).

The brain is more complex than a System 1 and System 2 process. It is more like an orchestra with different parts playing. All this exists in a whole body where each part affects the other. As you saw in chapter 6, you can prepare your body to calm your mind, and you can take steps to calm you mind to relax your body.

FIVE STAGES OF CHANGE

Imagine yourself on a raft moving along a river, in and out of a current. You drift into rapid waters. You glide over deep pools and scrape bottom in shallow waters. When you duck under low-hanging branches, you bump into a boulder. You paddle with your hands and kick with your feet. The current is strong. You can't easily go where you want. However, if you had a rudder and paddle, you could use the current to your advantage to get to the waypoints where you'd prefer to be.

The five stages of change map a process for self-mastery forged from meeting challenges, including intentionally paddling and steering to where you want to go. Here is what is involved:

1. *Awareness* is a typical starting point where you identify a problem area as well as your thoughts, feelings, and actions that relate to that area.

2. *Action* is the stage where you do something different to help bring about the change you want.

3. *Accommodation* follows when you alter your thinking, emotions, and actions in adapting to and integrating the change.

4. *Acceptance* is the emotional-integration phase of change. Your thinking, emotions, and actions are harmonious with a realistic perspective of events.

5. *Actualization* is where you make constructive new learnings a natural extension of what you do to serve your enlightened self-interests. You stretch to do better.

Change is a process, not an event. Although this may seem like a simplistic idea, the difference between a process and an event is as different as night and day. The five-stages process system will help you learn how to dull and then rid yourself of parasitic anger angles. Let's look at each more closely.

Awareness

Awareness refers to your conscious knowledge of how you are feeling and thinking and what motivates what you are doing. For example, what emotion(s) are you experiencing now? What is the content of your ongoing stream of thought? What is going on around you at this moment?

Intentional self-monitoring is a System 2 process. When you are in an anger-triggering situation and start to experience arousal and anger, your early awareness of parasitic anger thinking is an enormous advantage. You have a *Y* choice and options to divest yourself of that thinking before it boils over to aggression.

Action

You enter the action phase of change when you direct your actions to free yourself of a parasitic anger process. For example:

- You think about your thinking (metacognition) and identify anger-amplifying fictions like, *I can't stand it*. Once you recognize these thoughts, you can ask yourself what you mean by "it": *What is the "it" I'm telling myself I can't stand? Is "it" the feeling of tension I'm generating? Is there an aspect of the situation I especially don't like?*

- You bring parasitic thoughts into the sunlight by putting your attention onto them, saying them out loud (when you are by yourself), or writing them down. You are ready for the next step: questioning the validity of parasitic thoughts by cognitive reappraisal (see chapter 2) or by disputing irrational thinking (see chapter 3).

- When you know you are going to have a conflict, *mental rehearsal* is a tested way to simulate problem conditions to work on solutions. For example, you paid for quality work and materials, yet a contractor substituted substandard parts. The contractor is blameworthy for failing to live up to the contract. Decide what you want to accomplish. *Get your ducks lined up*. Rehearse different assertive scenarios.

Accommodation

System 2 is about knowing what is happening, acquiring information, and testing new ways of thinking and doing. *Accommodation* relates to adapting to accurate new information and to more effective ways of doing things.

Accommodation involves finding observations and information that are inconsistent with parasitic angry beliefs. Recognizing the disparities and knowing you can get past parasitic fallacies can both feel relieving and evoke tension. But it is a crucial step toward change.

When you've accommodated to helpful new information, you've made a System 2 change. However, System 1 irrationalities and impulses don't automatically vaporize under the weight of System 2 evidence and may remain, although in a weakened state, like silhouettes in the background of your mind. Under high-stress conditions, you might slip back to old ways of thinking and doing.

Recognizing how this duality principle (i.e., System 1 and System 2) works gives you another advantage. You need not heed false parasitic anger signals any more than you give ground to superstitious ones. Instead, you are free to decide to put your attention on what is wisest for you to do in any challenging situation.

Acceptance

Acceptance is an emotional-integration phase of change. You accept how you feel because that's how you feel. Emotional pulls and pushes remain. Accepting that System 1 assumptions based on fallacies can't automatically whipsaw you is an important discovery. You have a practiced, System 2 judgment you know you can exercise at *Y* choice points, where System 1 is heading for the quick and easy—yet self-defeating—path.

System 1 has legitimate powers that are part of who you are and what you do. Your intuition can be on the mark. You can anticipate based on what you perceive and be quite right. It's the snags, biases, and irrationalities that merit awareness and attention.

Personal change takes effort, and inner conflicts over the direction you'll take are inevitable. By accepting that duality, you'll have less of a struggle and, thus, less stress with that paradox of change.

Actualization

Actualization is where you stretch your abilities in sectors of your life where it is important for you to meet challenges and advance your enlightened self-interests. By selectively analyzing and thinking through situations, you learn more about what you can do and more about yourself as a result. Rather than seeking happiness, this and other emotive experiences are more of a byproduct of what you constructively do.

The advantage of stretching for excellence is that you are less likely to rest on your laurels, which is a formula for procrastinating and the inevitable stresses that go with delaying.

The horse and the rider, System 1 and System 2, and the raft on the river are metaphors that can help you at the point of a *Y* choice between following the automatic path or a deliberate one. Use whichever works best for you. Use all three!

MY FIVE-STAGE PROGRAM

Now it is your turn to use the five stages of change to put together a program to move forward on your journey toward reducing parasitic anger and its effects. In the table below, write down your answers to the questions pertaining to each of the five stages of change and how they apply to your life.

Awareness What do I need to know to reduce parasitic anger thinking? What's my incentive?	
Action What sequence of actions boosts my chances of bringing about a constructive result?	

Accommodation	
What incongruities between old parasitic and new productive ways of thinking can I benefit from resolving?	
Acceptance	
Emotions drive thoughts and actions, and vice versa. What are my options for creating a healthy congruity between these factors?	
Actualization	
In what ways can I stretch to learn more about myself and what I can accomplish?	

CHANGES BY RESTRICTIONS

What is freedom? Does freedom mean you can do whatever you want? If you yell and scream uncontrollably, does that show you are free? If so, then how does that differ from self-indulgence?

Freedom involves responsible restrictions. When you have a problem habit you want to change, you act to restrict yourself by doing something else. For example, you execute a System 2 effort to decrease parasitic extension-of-blame thinking by increasing the use of your rational thinking capabilities.

The idea of freedom by restriction is neither new nor unusual. You restrict yourself from expressing an unhealthy response by substituting a healthy one. So, if you want to lose weight, you substitute lower-calorie meals for supercharged-calorie meals. What better choice do you have?

The composer Igor Stravinsky saw restrictions as a means of freedom. You restrict yourself to what you want to do, and you free yourself to do that thing: "The more constraints one imposes, the more one frees oneself of the chains that shackle the spirit" (1947, 65). He freely created art in this way.

If you don't like the results you get from expressing angry impulses, can you restrict the impulses? If you ground the restriction in reason, you've taken a step toward freedom from an irrational restriction. Let's look at an unusual example where the concept of restrictions created freedom for a client of mine, a five-year-old girl named Julie (the concept is for people of all ages).

Julie had several problem behaviors, including throwing things in a grocery store and flinging food at her mother when she didn't get what she wanted to eat. The child had an anger problem and a high need for attention.

Out of frustration, her mother burned Julie with a hot iron. State authorities placed Julie in a temporary foster home. Meanwhile, both the mother and child had separate counselors. The goal was to get the family back together and functioning in a healthy way.

Shortly after I met Julie, I suggested a "let's pretend" game. She'd pretend she was in a grocery store, and she pretended to fling food from the grocery cart. I said it was my turn, and I pretended to push the cart and throw stuff from it. I said something like, "Wow. I'm happy. I won't have TV or dessert tonight." Julie quickly told me that wasn't supposed to happen.

I responded, "But isn't that what happens? If you want to lose TV and dessert, you do something. You throw groceries and food. You want something. You do something." Julie thought about that connection. She got it. After that, she restricted herself from throwing groceries and food. She enjoyed dessert and TV.

The idea that freedom comes with restrictions may seem strange. However, much depends on the restrictions you choose.

MY PROGRESS LOG

Key ideas: What three ideas did you pick up from this chapter that you found most helpful?

1.

2.

3.

Action plan: What three steps would you take to move closer to overcoming anger excesses?

1.

2.

3.

Execution: What are you going to do to execute the steps? (The process)

1.

2.

3.

Results: What do you hope to learn—or have reinforced—by taking these steps?

1.

2.

3.

Revisions: If you would make changes in the process, what would you do differently next time?

1.

2.

3.

CHAPTER 12

Top Tips from Anger Experts

When learning to successfully meet a major challenge, it helps to have input from different expert perspectives. In this final chapter, ten experts with lots of experience working with folks with anger problems share their top tips. If one tip makes a positive difference for you, this collective effort is worthwhile.

I suspect you'll pull from this chapter many useful ways to free yourself from parasitic anger that you can use to enjoy your life without this burden. You reserve the decision for yourself, of course, when it comes to deciding what makes the most sense for you to do.

TOP TIP: HARNESS THE POWER OF QUESTIONS

People are more likely to change when they have the tools to make the change and persist, persist, persist. This perspective can promote a positive self-fulfilling prophecy where you do what you think you can do. Toronto psychologist and author of *Pressure Proofing: How to Increase Personal Effectiveness*, Sam Klarreich, PhD, shares a question-and-answer approach for creating a positive self-fulfilling prophecy for overcoming excessive anger. Here's Klarreich's tip.

Chronic anger is a silent killer that repeatedly produces surges of stress hormones, such as cortisol, which stimulates the production of plaque on the inside lining of your arteries. A plaque buildup elevates your risk for coronary heart disease and stroke.

You can reduce health risks, have fewer fractured relationships, and feel better inside with less anger. Here are four sample questions and answers my angry clients found helpful in their trek of breaking free from the kinds of damaging anger that can quickly grow out of proportion.

Question	Answer	How Can You Use This Information?	Result from New Actions
What do you typically tell yourself that triggers your anger?			
If you believe you have no choice but to get aggressive when frustrated, would you teach kindergarten children how to explode in anger if they didn't get their way?			
If you usually blame others, what problems does that solve for you?			
What's the most compelling argument to challenge your anger thinking?			

TOP TIP: PREPARE FOR PROVOCATIONS AND FRUSTRATIONS

Relaxation and imagery are scientifically proven to reduce stress. These techniques arise from the work of Joseph Wolpe (1973), who showed how progressive relaxation actions can calm stresses and strains. Likewise, imagery, such as viewing a beautiful stream in the woods, has been shown to be an effective antidote to stress.

William L. Golden, PhD, a psychologist in private practice in Briarcliff Manor, New York, an author, and an REBT (rational emotive behavior therapy) training supervisor, tells how to practice and then use relaxation and imagery to cope effectively in provocative and frustrating situations using an "RICP" method he developed.

Normal frustrations with other people's behaviors are inevitable. The range of problem situations can seem unlimited. If your frustrations about people cascade into anger thinking and problematic reactions, how do you prepare yourself to break this pattern?

RICP is a way to slow down and respond effectively in provocative situations. In RICP, *R* stands for relaxation, *I* for imagery of a provocative situation, *C* for coping statements, and *P* for a problem-solving response. You can put RICP to work for you when you have a legitimate gripe. Let's look at an example.

Eric was an avid movie fan. As if programmed this way, Eric felt angry to the point of hostility toward people who talked during a movie. Here is what Eric practiced to help himself stop souring his movie-going experiences.

In thinking about his thinking, Eric identified a sequence of angry thoughts: People should be more polite. These creeps should be more considerate. *Now he felt justified in his belief that* rude people should be told off. *To see if he could avoid verbal confrontations and fights that occasionally resulted from telling people off, he decided to relax his body and mind and try a different way. Here is the RICP program that Eric practiced.*

Relaxation	Imagery	Coping Statements	Problem Solving
Eric focused on breathing in and out deeply and slowly. He thought the word "calm" as he created a calming feeling.	Maintaining deep breathing, he imagined himself at a theater with people behind him talking. He found that the feeling of calm continued.	Before he started the exercise, Eric had devised coping statements. While continuing deep breathing and imagining the provocative situation, he evoked these thoughts. Here is an example: *I wish people would be polite and not talk during movies, but it's unrealistic to expect it.* His feeling of calm remained.	Eric had a practical problem to solve. While continuing deep breathing, he imagined calmly telling the talkers he would appreciate it if they would stop talking so he could enjoy the movie.

Over the next several days, Eric practiced RICP fifty times. When he next went to the movies, he purposefully sat near three people who appeared to be friends actively engaged in conversation. Eric practiced deep breathing. He let the word "calm" flow though his mind. When the movie started, the friends talked loudly to each other at times. Eric engaged RICP. Then he pleasantly asked if they might stop talking as he'd like to hear the movie. He got a polite response: "Sure, no problem. Sorry."

On another occasion, a group of people sat in front of him. They started talking. Eric went through his RICP exercise. Then he heard them planning to beat up on a person named Larry. They sounded like they were itching for a fight. Previously he would have let his angry feelings overtake his reason. This time he sought a problem-solving alternative. Eric moved to another seat.

If you think RICP is workable for you, think of a situation that typically angers you, and complete the boxes below with your responses.

Relaxation	Imagery	Coping Statements	Problem Solving

TOP TIP: REALIGN THE COSTS AND BENEFITS OF YOUR ANGER

Russell Grieger, PhD, is a clinical psychologist in private practice, an organizational consultant, an adjunct professor at the University of Virginia, and the author of numerous books based on REBT, his latest being *The Serious Business of Being Happy: A Cognitive Behavior Workbook to Bring Happiness to Every Day of Life* (2020). Dr. Grieger provides a useful exercise to do a cost-benefit analysis of being angry.

If you suffered from anxiety or depression, you'd be happy to free yourself from these feelings. Anger is different. You may resist freeing yourself from automatic, cognitive, harmful forms of anger because they are challenging to relinquish. You may experience a sense of power that can do you more harm than good. The following two-step cost-benefit analysis experiment can give you an added incentive for reducing harmful anger.

COST-BENEFIT ANALYSIS OF MY ANGER

Step One: List the benefits and costs of both being and not being angry. The following chart shows a sample analysis.

Issues	Benefits	Costs
Being Angry	I put others in their place. I feel powerful and energized when I'm angrily lashing out.	It sours relationships. People act revengefully. I act impulsively and cause more problems for myself.
Not Being Angry	Can show wiser judgment in problem-solving situations. Can keep emotionally centered. Can change anger-evoking beliefs that distort my views on life.	Time on the task of refining and practicing personal problem-solving skills. Time on the task of learning to monitor my thoughts and accurately reappraise conditions to sharpen my perspective. Time and effort developing a reasonable and realistic perspective on myself, other people, and life.

Here is a chart for your use:

Issues	Benefits	Costs
Being Angry		
Not Being Angry		

Step Two: Project yourself into the future. Using the content in the above charts, visualize the cost of a lifetime of feeling impulsively driven by anger. Visualize the life benefits of lessening or breaking automatic anger patterns. Repeat this exercise daily for ten days. Does this assessment give you an extra incentive to experiment with ways to free yourself from the costs of living with needless anger?

TOP TIP: DETERMINE WHETHER YOUR EXPECTATIONS MATCH REALITY

When your expectations fail to match the results, frustration occurs. This is a normal event in everyday life. What is not normal is getting angry over the gap between expectation and result. Getting yourself into the habit of having realistic expectations and knowing that the results won't always match can be an effective antidote to angry responses that add to needless stresses and strains.

Elliot D. Cohen, PhD, author of *Making Peace with Imperfection: Discover Your Perfectionism Type, End the Cycle of Criticism, and Embrace Self-Acceptance* (2019), provides a quick tip to help manage our expectations.

Are you an *expectation perfectionist*? Expectation perfectionists judge the worthiness of others based on whether or not they live up to their perfectionistic expectations. If you *demand* that others behave as you expect, and then they fail to do so (as they eventually will), you may rate *them* as worthless or bad persons and treat them in ways you will later regret. *He was supposed to signal before he got into my lane—that no-good, worthless, piece of garbage.* Road rage, battery, domestic violence, and even murder may be consequences of such perfectionistic expectations. First, practice changing these expectations to preferences (*I prefer that others satisfy my standards, but I know this won't always happen*). Second, stick to rating the actions of others when they fall short, not the persons themselves (*What he did was a bad thing, but that does mean* he *is a bad thing*). In this way, you will give yourself an opportunity to rationally address the perceived mistake.

TOP TIP: WATCH YOURSELF THROUGH THE MIRROR

The song "Put on a Happy Face" was about gloomy days and faces of gloom. The song carried a positive message of smiling your troubles way. By changing your facial expression to a smile, you can alter an angry mood as well. Let's see how.

Roberta Galluccio Richardson, PhD, AFBPsS, treats adults and children in her New York City practice and uses short-term cognitive behavioral therapy (CBT), which is practical and effective, as shown by many clinical studies. Dr. Richardson provides helpful information about the thoughts that accompany anger and how these affect overall health.

If you experience frequent bouts of anger, you are likely to have negative thoughts accompanied by an elevated heartbeat and higher blood pressure. Did you know that habitual angry thoughts and feelings also affect your blood glucose levels, increase the likelihood of experiencing headaches and migraines, decrease blood flow in your digestive system, and put your long-term health at risk?

Risk doesn't mean certainty. You could escape all health, personal, and social consequences of anger. But why gamble when you don't have to? As an alternative, you could decide to reduce anger-triggering negative thoughts, reduce anger-related health risks, and improve the quality of your life. That typically takes doing many things to help achieve this outcome. That's the path of problem prevention, and it is a solid path to follow.

You have many ways to prevent and reduce anger. Here is a pleasant, simple-to-do, early-morning experiment than can help lower the risk for anger tensions and improve your chances for experiencing pleasant sensations. The experiment consists of looking into the mirror and smiling. If that seems odd, don't worry. You are not alone in thinking that. However, you can do this in a natural way every day by tweaking one thing that you do.

Put your face into a smile while brushing your teeth. The tweaking lies in being mindful of allowing your facial expression to trigger positive feelings. This is feasible because how you posture yourself and the facial expressions you create can evoke feelings that typically go with the expression. The experiment is to find out how often you experience a positive feeling when you intentionally smile while brushing your teeth.

When you feel positive, negative thoughts fade. You are less likely to start your day looking for a fight. So, start your day with a smile. You may find others smiling back at you.

TOP TIP: SWITCH ON THE RIGHT-BRAIN CIRCUITS

To turn on a light, you use a switch. The idea applies when switching from the dark underside of anger to an enlightened view. Here the switch is different. This is more like a rheostat, or regulator. Exercise can act like a switch, or rheostat. Fortunately, you have other rheostats at your disposal to down-regulate needless anger. Here is a potpourri of options.

Pamela D. Garcy, PhD, psychologist and author of *The REBT Super-Activity Guide: 52 Weeks of REBT for Clients, Groups, Students, and YOU!* (2009), provides a tip to switch off angry outbursts through healthy activities. It's hard to feel angry while jogging in a scenic park. It is unlikely you will feel angry while listening to one of your favorite Mozart concertos.

Here's Garcy's tip: First, disengage your angry brain and engage your thinking brain. Rather than having an outburst, you'll instead want to take actions to quell the burst of emotions and your body's physical responses. To reduce your angry brain's "fight" response:

1. Switch to "healthy flight" using a physical release. Examples include jogging, walking, swimming, throwing ice to the ground, and shooting hoops.

2. Switch to "healthy freeze" using soothing and healthy self-expression. Examples of soothing include gentle stretching, taking a shower, breathing deeply, practicing mindfulness, talking to a soothing person, listening to calming music, drinking a cup of chamomile tea, smelling lavender, and reading. Examples of healthy self-expression include writing a blog or poem, drawing, dancing, singing, and playing music.

Next, restore your mood using your thinking brain:

1. Ask yourself, *Is this an emergency, irritation, or glitch? Is it a problem I can solve, or one I can only cope with?*

2. Use "Even if" to acknowledge the challenge.

3. Use "I prefer and will work toward" to acknowledge what you want and can work on.

4. Use "I'm making myself angry by" to acknowledge your power.

5. Use "Always" to show yourself the absurdity of your angry brain's *shoulds*.

Below is an example of how to use these five steps:

1. Another driver swoops into a parking spot you were aiming for. You ask yourself, *Is this an emergency? No. Is this an irritation? Yes. Is this a glitch? Yes.* Now that you know it's an irritation and a glitch, it's easier to calmly move to another parking spot. That's a problem I can cope with.

2. *Even if* this is an irritation and a glitch, I can choose to calmly take it in stride. No emergency exists and all will be okay.

3. *I prefer and will work toward* calmly accepting an irritating glitch in what I would prefer (having that parking spot).

4. *I'm making myself angry by* thinking negative thoughts about the "rotten so-and-so who rudely stole my spot." I can choose to allow myself to realize that, although irritated, I can handle getting another spot quite easily.

5. *He always tries to take a spot I'm aiming for, and he's the worst rotten human being on Earth. He should rot in hell for eternity.* The absurdity of this angry brain thought can help reduce the anger to quiet resolve.

TOP TIP: PRACTICE 3-D RATIONAL EMOTIVE IMAGERY

As you go through life, you'll occasionally find a wise person with an answer to a question that had puzzled you. You'll also find people who took the advice and can advise you on how it worked for them. What follows is how to put into action advice from a master.

Shawn Blau, PhD (ATR Advisors LLC, Westport, CT 06880), coeditor of *The Albert Ellis Reader: A Guide to Well-Being Using Rational Emotive Behavior Therapy* (Ellis and Blau 1998), provides an important tip about using 3-D rational emotive imagery:

Albert Ellis himself taught this to me in 1987. It worked like a charm, and I've used it ever since. First, pick an unfair situation in which you tend to make yourself angry, or an unfair person at whom you tend to anger yourself. Then use rational emotive imagery (REI) to imagine yourself getting very angry, and then work at staying in this unfair situation but changing your anger to a more coping emotion. Once you have attained mastery over your anger in REI, seek out and actually court the unfair person or situation that you imagined in imagery. Rehearse your previously practiced REI (1) before the interaction, (2) during the interaction, and (3) after the interaction. Push yourself to do this in vivo (in real life) as often as possible. Within a very few weeks, you will find yourself in much more control of your anger than you ever thought possible.

TOP TIP: APPLY EMPATHY AND PERSPECTIVE FOR ANGER REDUCTION

Empathy is built into human nature. This sense of understanding others' feelings has therapeutic value in promoting a sense of acceptance between people. It's tough to be raging at someone while simultaneously feeling empathy for them. Let's see how to tip the scale in an empathy direction.

Here is advice from Howard Kassinove, professor emeritus at Hofstra University and coauthor of Tafrate and Kassinove's (2019) *Anger Management for Everyone* and Kassinove and Tafrate's (2019) *The Practitioner's Guide to Anger Management*. He provides a tip for using empathy and perspective to reduce anger.

Anger is typically caused by the actions of others that are perceived to be unwanted, inappropriate, unhelpful, or wrong. You may feel angry when your child, who is underachieving, repeatedly plays computer games after being asked to study. Or your spouse might repeatedly buy lottery tickets after promising to not do so. The anger, bitterness, and vengeance you feel is bad for *you* and does not help *you* develop solutions to such problems.

The roadblock is that we all see the world from our own perspective. If your child keeps playing those video games excessively, you focus on how *you* are being disrespected. If your spouse continues to buy those tickets, you focus on how *you* are being insulted and you continue to angrily blame your spouse for the purchases.

One way to reduce your anger is to minimize blaming and become more empathic—that is, to understand the behavior from the other person's perspective. Once empathy is achieved, anger naturally diminishes and opportunities for problem resolution open up.

Perspective taking is one way to encourage empathy and reduce anger. It has four steps.

1. In the quiet of your home, silently recall the situation that led to your anger. Do not exaggerate or minimize what happened. Limit your review to the specific situation.

2. While alone, describe aloud what happened. Do it from your perspective, as though you are talking to a friend. Wait a few minutes.

3. Now, switch and pretend to be the other person. Describe the situation from that person's perspective. Again, while alone, talk aloud as though you are that other person who is now talking to you. Describe what happened and generate possible, legitimate, and realistic reasons as to why you (as the other person) acted as you did. Importantly, use "I" language and talk as though you are that other person.

4. Repeat three times.

The more you understand the other person's perspective, the quicker your anger will be reduced and you can then move forward to either find solutions or forgive. You will no longer be the angry and bitter victim of the other person's actions.

TOP TIP: STOP AND THINK IT OUT

Licensed psychologist Diana R. Richman, PhD, maintains a private practice in New York City. A graduate postdoctoral fellow and former faculty member of the Albert Ellis Institute, she has authored numerous articles on the application of REBT and CBT to life stages and work-related issues.

Do you believe that you can and/or want to overcome feeling angry? Mindfully acknowledging your honest answer to this question will motivate you to challenge the cognitive blocks to overcome this often unnecessary, self-defeating emotion. If you desire to reduce your angry feelings, the following series of tips will help you to move forward as you live in this realistically unfair world.

1. Clarify the *object of your anger*. Do you feel the emotion of anger toward a person, a situation, and/or yourself?

   - This step may be achieved by acknowledging that you believe someone and/or some situation is to *blame* for your strong emotion.

2. Clarify if you honestly want to overcome feeling the emotion of anger. Do you believe that your anger is *justified*?

   - This step may be achieved by acknowledging that you have a *choice* to overcome the emotion of anger, even when believing that the activating event was *unjustified, and therefore your anger is justified.*

3. Clarify the *specific beliefs* that you maintain about the object of your anger. Do you believe your thoughts evoke your anger?

   - This step may be achieved by *challenging your maintained unrealistic expectations* and resulting blame toward yourself, others, and situations, regardless of life realities.

4. Clarify the *intensity* of your angry emotion on a scale from 0 (no anger) to 10 (severe anger).

   - This step may be achieved by *monitoring* your emotion a consistent number of times per day and writing the date, time, and intensity from 0 to 10.

5. Clarify the *advantages and disadvantages* of reducing the emotion of anger. Do you benefit from reducing your angry feelings?

   - This step may be achieved by making a two-column list of the advantages and disadvantages of maintaining this negative, painful emotion and allowing your thoughts to consider the *long-term benefits of letting go* of your angry feelings.

6. Clarify that you can *forgive* yourself, others, and situations to free yourself from this long-standing, self-defeating emotion.

   - This step may be achieved by recognizing that forgiveness *frees you to move on* in your life to healthy, self-enhancing goals.

TOP TIP: RECOGNIZE THAT YOU HAVE A CHOICE

Fortunately, you have quite a few good choices when it comes to overcoming anger. A first step is becoming aware of them. Norman Cotterell, PhD, of the Beck Institute for Cognitive Behavior Therapy, wraps up our top tips with his famous AWARE plan for healthy and constructive choices and behaviors in reducing anger.

The first step in dealing with anger is to recognize choice. There are a myriad of things we don't control: the past, other people, intrusive thoughts, physical sensations, even emotions. But there is something within these that we absolutely do control: our ability to choose. We choose what we learn from the past, how to respond to other people, and what we do in the context of intrusive thoughts, feelings, and urges. Importantly, we can choose whether to focus on the things we don't control or the things we do control.

A useful technique in recognizing such choice is a simple cost-benefit analysis. Envision someone who handles anger in a way that you respect and admire. Let's call him Mike. What words would you use to describe his style? Controlled? Accepting? Forgiving? Whatever word applies, write it down. Then ask yourself four questions: *What are the disadvantages of being like Mike? What are the advantages of being angry? What are the disadvantages of being angry?* And finally, *What are the advantages of being like Mike?* Then ask: *Do the benefits of anger outweigh the costs? Are they about equal? Or do the costs of anger outweigh the benefits?* Weigh them if you'd like: 50-50, 55-45, 60-40, 70-30, 80-20, 90-10, or 100-0? Then, do the same with the costs and benefits of being like Mike.

Note that the costs of anger may really be the costs of aggression (or passive-aggression, or even passivity). We may not control anger, but we have full control over what we do with anger. We can be angry and aggressive, angry and passive-aggressive, angry and passive, or angry and assertive. It's our choice. Anger can quicken our reactions and make it seem like no choice is involved. Still, we need to empower ourselves by regarding these options as choices.

So, remember and be AWARE:

Accept anger: It doesn't mean you are out of control. It is energy to problem solve—at best, to do the right thing in the right way in the service of your values.

Watch it from a distance: It is energy to help you deal with a challenging situation. It is your choice what to do with it.

Act constructively with it: Use it in the service of your morals and values. Strive for compassion, patience, understanding, empathy, and grace.

Repeat the above: Continue to accept, watch, and act constructively with it.

Expect the best: It is temporary.

TYING IT ALL TOGETHER: WHAT MATTERS IN LIFE

This book has much to say about meaning: the meaning you give to events, the meaning you give to your emotions, and the meaning embedded in your beliefs. Let's finish with the meaning you give to your life.

Engaging in what matters helps make life meaningful. That's a path to emotional well-being and health (Costin and Vignoles 2020). What are these things that matter? For some, family and friends matter most. Others dive into areas of personal interest when they can. Some take time to defend those who can't protect themselves. Others do multiple things that matter, such as write stories, create gardens, and restore old stuff. Some build businesses. For some rare persons, their work is their magnificent obsession. Albert Ellis worked tirelessly for decades passionately pursuing the development of his REBT system seven days a week for about sixty years. What he accomplished mattered, not only to him, but also to millions who used his system and others who pull from his wisdom, now merged into CBT.

You may not know what matters for strangers who cross your life for a moment. Here is what I learned from a stranger on a subway train. He was a messenger who told me about what cars to ride, so I would be near to the stairs when the train stopped and save time. Efficiency is what mattered to him. He was full of enthusiasm about this.

Next time you head toward a parasitic anger mindset about an event, pause. What are you grateful for having as a part of your life? Doesn't that matter more?

References

Alberti, R., and M. Emmons. 1970. *Your Perfect Right*. 1st ed. San Luis Obispo, CA: Impact Publishers.

Alberti, R., and M. Emmons. 2017. *Your Perfect Right*. 10th ed. Oakland, CA: Impact Publishers.

Alexandru, B. V., B. Róbert, L. Viorel, and B. Vasile. 2009. "Treating Primary Insomnia: A Comparative Study of Self-Help Methods and Progressive Muscle Relaxation." *Journal of Cognitive and Behavioral Psychotherapies* 9 (1): 67–82.

American Psychological Association. 2017. "Stress in America: The State of Our Nation." *Stress in America Survey*.

Aristotle. 1999. (Translated by W. D. Ross). *Nicomachean Ethics*. Kitchener Canada: Batoche Books.

Ariyabuddhiphongs, V. 2014. "Anger Concepts and Anger Reduction Method in Theravada Buddhism." *Spirituality in Clinical Practice* 1 (1): 56–66.

Aspinwall, L. G. 2011. Future-oriented Thinking, Proactive Coping, and the Management of Potential Threats to Health and Well-being. In S. Folkman (ed.), *Oxford Library of Psychology. The Oxford Handbook of Stress, Health, and Coping* (334–365). New York, NY: Oxford University Press.

Bear, G. G., X. Uribe-Zarain, M. A. Manning, and K. Shiomi. 2009. "Shame, Guilt, Blaming, and Anger: Differences Between Children in Japan and the US." *Motivation and Emotion* 33 (3): 229–238.

Beck, A. 1999. *Prisoners of Hate*. New York: Harper Collins.

Bekoff, M., and J. Pierce. 2009. *The Moral Lives of Animals*. Chicago: University of Chicago Press.

Belenky, G., N. J. Wesensten, D. R. Thorne, M. L. Thomas, H. C. Sing, D. P. Redmond, M. B. Russo, and T. J. Balkin. 2003. "Patterns of Performance Degradation and Restoration During Sleep Restriction and Subsequent Recovery: A Sleep Dose-Response Study." *Journal of Sleep Research* 12 (1): 1–12.

Berkowitz, L. 1990. "On the Formation and Regulation of Anger and Aggression: A Cognitive-Neoassociationistic Analysis." *American Psychologist* 45 (4): 494–503.

Beute, F., and Y. A. W. de Kort. 2018. "The Natural Context of Wellbeing: Ecological Momentary Assessment of the Influence of Nature and Daylight on Affect and Stress for Individuals with Depression Levels Varying from None to Clinical." *Health and Place* 49: 7–18.

Block, J. 2018. *The 15-Minute Relationship Fix: A Clinically Proven Strategy that Will Repair and Strengthen Your Love Life*. Virginia Beach, VA: Koehler Books.

Boesch, C. 2002. "Cooperative Hunting Roles Among Taï Chimpanzees." *Human Nature* 13 (1): 27–46.

Bothelius, K., K. Kyhle, C. A. Espie, and J. E. Broman. 2013. "Manual-Guided Cognitive–Behavioural Therapy for Insomnia Delivered by Ordinary Primary Care Personnel in General Medical Practice: A Randomized Controlled Effectiveness Trial." *Journal of Sleep Research* 22 (6): 688–696.

Bourland, D. D. and P. D. Johnston. 1991. *To Be or Not: An E-Prime Anthology.* San Francisco: International Society for General Semantics.

Brehm, S. S., and J. W. Brehm. 1981. *Psychological Reactance: A Theory of Freedom and Control.* New York: Academic Press.

Brosnan, S. F., and F. B. M. de Waal. 2003. "Monkeys Reject Unequal Pay." *Nature* 425 (6955): 297–299.

Buhle, J. T., J. A. Silvers, T. D. Wager, R. Lopez, C. Onyemekwu, H. Kober, and K. N. Ochsner. 2014. "Cognitive Reappraisal of Emotion: A Meta-Analysis of Human Neuroimaging Studies." *Cerebral Cortex* 24 (11): 2981–2990.

Busch, L. Y., P. Pössel, and J. C. Valentine. 2017. "Meta-Analyses of Cardiovascular Reactivity to Rumination: A Possible Mechanism Linking Depression and Hostility to Cardiovascular Disease." *Psychological Bulletin* 143 (12): 1378–1394.

Buschmann, T., R. A. Horn, V. R. Blankenship, Y. E. Garcia, and K. B. Bohan. 2018. "The Relationship Between Automatic Thoughts and Irrational Beliefs Predicting Anxiety and Depression." *Journal of Rational-Emotive & Cognitive-Behavior Therapy* 36 (2):137–162.

Bushman, B. J. 2002. "Does Venting Anger Feed or Extinguish the Flame? Catharsis, Rumination, Distraction, Anger and Aggressive Responding." *Personality and Social Psychology Bulletin* 28 (6): 724–773.

Carlsmith, K. M., T. D. Wilson, and D. T. Gilbert. 2008. "The Paradoxical Consequences of Revenge." *Journal of Personality and Social Psychology* 95 (6): 1316–1324.

Carter, C. L. 2009. Consumer Protection in the States. National Consumer Law Center. www.nclc.org.

Caselli, G., A. Offredi, F. Martino, D. Varalli, G. M. Ruggiero, S. Sassaroli, M. M. Spada, and A. Wells. 2017. "Metacognitive Beliefs and Rumination as Predictors of Anger: A Prospective Study." *Aggressive Behavior* 43 (5): 421–429.

Casriel, D. 1974. *A Scream Away from Happiness.* New York: Grossett and Dunlap.

Cassiello-Robbins, C., and D. H. Barlow. 2016. "Anger: The Unrecognized Emotion in Emotional Disorders." *Clinical Psychology: Science and Practice* 23 (1): 66–85.

Chester, D. S., and J. M. Dzierzewski. 2019. "Sour Sleep, Sweet Revenge? Aggressive Pleasure as a Potential Mechanism Underlying Poor Sleep Quality's Link to Aggression." *Emotion.* Advance online publication.

Chida, Y., and A. Steptoe. 2009. "Cortisol Awakening Response and Psychosocial Factors: A Systematic Review and Meta-Analysis." *Biological Psychology* 80 (3): 265–278.

Clark, G. and S. J. Egan. 2015. "The Socratic Method in Cognitive Behavioural Therapy: A Narrative Review." *Cognitive Therapy and Research* 39 (6): 863–879.

Coccaro, E. F. 2019. Psychiatric Comorbidity in Intermittent Explosive Disorder. *Journal of Psychiatric Research* 118: 38–43.

Cohen, E. 2019. *Making Peace with Imperfection: Discover Your Perfectionism Type, End the Cycle of Criticism, and Embrace Self-Acceptance.* Oakland, CA: Impact Publishers.

Cooley, C. H. 1902. *Human Nature and the Social Order.* New York: Scribner.

Costin, V., and V. L. Vignoles. 2020. "Meaning Is About Mattering: Evaluating Coherence, Purpose, and Existential Mattering as Precursors of Meaning in Life Judgments." *Journal of Personality and Social Psychology* 118 (4): 864–884.

Damasio, A. 2017. *The Strange Order of Things.* New York: Vintage Books.

David, D., C. Cotet, S. Matu, C. Mogoase, and S. Stefan. 2018. "50 Years of Rational-Emotive and Cognitive-Behavioral Therapy: A Systematic Review and Meta-Analysis." *Journal of Clinical Psychology* 74 (3): 304–318.

Davidson K. W., and E. Mostofsky. 2010. "Anger Expression and Risk of Coronary Heart Disease: Evidence from the Nova Scotia Health Survey." *American Heart Journal* 158 (2): 199–206.

Deak, M. C., and R. Stickgold. 2010. "Sleep and Cognition." *WIREs Cognitive Science* 1 (4): 491–500.

De Couck, M., R. Caers, L. Musch, J. Fliegauf, A. Giangreco, and Y. Gidron. 2019. "How Breathing Can Help You Make Better Decisions: Two Studies on the Effects of Breathing Patterns on Heart Rate Variability And Decision-Making In Business Cases." *International Journal of Psychophysiology* 139: 1–9.

Denny, B. T., and K. N. Ochsner. 2014. "Behavioral Effects of Longitudinal Training in Cognitive Reappraisal." *Emotion* 14 (2): 425–433.

Dor, D. 2017. "The Role of the Lie in the Evolution of Human Language." *Language Sciences* 63: 44–59.

Dubois, P. 1909a. *The Psychic Treatment of Nervous Disorders.* New York: Funk & Wagnalls.

Dubois, P. 1909b. *The Psychic Treatment of Nervous Disorders.* 6th ed. New York: Funk & Wagnalls.

Dunlap, K. 1949. *Habits: Their Making and Unmaking.* New York: Liveright Publishing.

D'Zurilla, T. J., and M. R. Goldfried. 1971. "Problem Solving and Behavior Modification." *Journal of Abnormal Psychology* 78 (1): 107–126.

Eadeh, F. R., S. A. Peak, and A. J. Lambert. 2017. "The Bittersweet Taste of Revenge: On the Negative and Positive Consequences of Retaliation." *Journal of Experimental Social Psychology* 68: 27–39.

Ellis, A. 1962. *Reason and Emotion in Psychotherapy.* New York: Lyle Stuart.

Ellis, A. 1977. *How to Live with and without Anger.* New York: Reader's Digest Press.

Ellis, A. 1999. *How to Make Yourself Happy and Remarkably Less Disturbable*. Oakland, CA: Impact Publishers.

Ellis, A. and S. Blau. 1998. *Albert Ellis Reader*. Secaucus, New Jersey: Citadel Press.

Eriksson, K., P. A. Andersson, and P. Strimling. 2017. "When Is It Appropriate to Reprimand a Norm Violation? The Roles of Anger, Behavioral Consequences, Violation Severity, and Social Distance." *Judgment and Decision Making* 12 (4): 396–407.

Fahlgren, M. K., A. A. Puhalla, K. M. Sorgi, and M. S. McCloskey. 2019. "Emotion Processing in Intermittent Explosive Disorder." *Psychiatry Research* 273: 544–550.

Felt, J. M., M. A. Russell, J. M. Ruiz, J. A. Johnson, B. N. Uchino, M. Allison, T. W. Smith, D. J. Taylor, C. Ahn, and J. Smyth. 2020. "A Multimethod Approach Examining the Relative Contributions of Optimism and Pessimism to Cardiovascular Disease Risk Markers." *Journal of Behavioral Medicine*. https://doi.org/10.1007/s10865-020-00133-6

Ford, B. Q., P. Lam, O. P. John, and I. B. Mauss. 2018. "The Psychological Health Benefits of Accepting Negative Emotions and Thoughts: Laboratory, Diary, and Longitudinal Evidence." *Journal of Personality and Social Psychology* 115 (6): 1075–1092.

Frankl, V. 1988. *The Will to Meaning*. New York: Meridian.

Friedrich, A., and A. A. Schlarb. 2018. "Let's Talk about Sleep: A Systematic Review of Psychological Interventions to Improve Sleep in College Students." *Journal of Sleep Research* 27 (1): 4–22.

Gabay, A. S., J. Radua, M. J. Kempton, and M. A. Mehta. 2014. "The Ultimatum Game and the Brain: A Meta-Analysis of Neuroimaging Studies." *Neuroscience and Biobehavioral Reviews* 47: 549–558.

Gao, L., J. Curtiss, X. Liu, and S. G. Hofmann. 2018. "Differential Treatment Mechanisms in Mindfulness Meditation and Progressive Muscle Relaxation." *Mindfulness* 9 (4): 1316–1317.

Garcy, P. 2009. *The REBT Super-Activity Guide: 52 Weeks of REBT for Clients, Groups, Students, and YOU!* CreateSpace Independent Publishing Platform.

Geraci, A., and L. Surian. 2011. "The Developmental Roots of Fairness: Infants' Reactions to Equal and Unequal Distributions of Resources." *Developmental Science* 14 (5): 1012–1020.

Graver, M. 2007. *Stoicism and Emotion*. Chicago: The University of Chicago Press.

Gray. C. 2002. *A Study of State Judicial Discipline Sanctions*. Chicago: American Judicial Society.

Greenglass, E. 1996. "Anger Suppression, Cynical Distrust, and Hostility: Implications for Coronary Heart Disease." In *Stress and Emotion: Anxiety, Anger, and Curiosity*, Vol. 16, edited by C. D. Spielberger, I. G. Sarason, J. M. T. Brebner, and guest editors E. Greenglass, P. Laungani, and A. M. O'Roark, 205–225. Washington, DC: Taylor and Francis.

Grieger, R. 2020. *The Serious Business of Being Happy*. New York: Routledge.

Haesevoets, T., D. De Cremer, A. Van Hiel, and F. Van Overwalle. 2018. "Understanding the Positive Effect of Financial Compensation on Trust After Norm Violations: Evidence from fMRI in Favor of Forgiveness." *Journal of Applied Psychology* 103 (5):578–590.

Harinck, F., and G. A. Van Kleef. 2012. "Be Hard on the Interests and Soft on the Values: Conflict Issue Moderates the Effects of Anger in Negotiations." *British Journal of Social Psychology* 51 (4): 741–72.

Heiniger, L. E., G. I. Clark, and S. J. Egan. 2017. "Perceptions of Socratic and Non-Socratic Presentation of Information in Cognitive Behaviour Therapy." *Journal of Behavior Therapy and Experimental Psychiatry* 58: 106–113.

Hofmann, S. 2020. *The Anxiety Skills Workbook*. Oakland, CA: New Harbinger Publications.

Hofmann, S. G., and G. J. G. Asmundson, eds. 2017. *The Science of Cognitive Behavioral Therapy*. San Diego, CA: Elsevier Academic Press.

Horney, K. 1950. *Neurosis and Human Growth*. New York: W. W. Norton & Company, Inc.

Hosseini, S. H., V. Mokhberi, R. A. Mohammadpour, M. Mehrabianfard, and L. N. Lashak. 2011. "Anger Expression and Suppression Among Patients with Essential Hypertension." *International Journal of Psychiatry in Clinical Practice* 15: 214–218.

Jackobson, E. 1938. *Progressive Relaxation*. 2nd ed. Chicago: University of Chicago Press.

Janicki-Deverts, D., S. Cohen, and W. Doyle. 2010. "Cynical Hostility and Stimulated Th1 and Th2 Cytokine Production." *Brain Behavior Immunology* 24 (1): 58–63.

Janov, A. 1975. *The Primal Scream*. New York: Dell Publishing.

Jones, M. C. 1924. "A Laboratory Study of Fear: The Case of Peter." *The Pedagogical Seminary* 31 (4): 308–315.

Jones, V. C. 1948. *The Hatfields and the McCoys*. Chapel Hill North Carolina: University of North Carolina Press.

Julkunen, J., P. R. Salonen, J. A. Kaplan, M. A. Chesney, and J. T. Salonen. 1994. "Hostility and the Progression of Carotid Atherosclerosis." *Psychosomatic Medicine* 56: 519–525.

Kabat-Zinn, J. 2005. *Coming to Our Senses*. New York: Hyperion.

Kahneman, D. 2011. *Thinking Fast and Slow*. New York: Farrar, Straus and Giroux.

Kassinove, H., and C. Tafrate. 2019. *The Practitioner's Guide to Anger Management*. Oakland, CA: New Harbinger Publications.

Kazantzis, N., H. K. Luong, A. S. Usatoff, T. Impala, R. Y. Yew, and S. G. Hofmann. 2018. "The Processes of Cognitive Behavioral Therapy: A Review of Meta-Analyses." *Cognitive Therapy and Research* 42 (4): 349–357.

Kelly, G. 1969. "The Strategy of Psychological Research." In *Clinical Psychology and Personality: The Collected Papers of George Kelly,* edited by B. Maher. New York: John Wiley and Sons.

Kelly, G. 1955. *The Psychology of Personal Constructs.* New York: W. W. Norton & Company, Inc.

Kessler, R. C., E. F. Coccaro, M. Fava, S. Jaeger, R. Jin, and E. Walters. 2006. "The Prevalence and Correlates of DSM-IV Intermittent Explosive Disorder in the National Comorbidity Survey Replication." *Archives of General Psychiatry* 63 (6): 669–678.

Kim, Y. J. 2018. "Transdiagnostic Mechanism of Social Phobia and Depression: The Role of Anger Dysregulation." *Journal of Human Behavior in the Social Environment* 28 (8): 1048–1059.

King, R. B., and E. D. dela Rosa. 2019. "Are Your Emotions under Your Control or Not? Implicit Theories of Emotion Predict Well-Being via Cognitive Reappraisal." *Personality and Individual Differences* 139: 177–182.

Klarreich, S. 2007. *Pressure Proofing: How to Increase Personal Effectiveness on the Job and Anywhere Else for that Matter.* New York: Routledge.

Kline, C. E. 2019. "Sleep and Exercise." In M. A. Grandner (ed.), *Sleep and Health* (257–267). Burlington, Massachusetts: Elsevier Academic Press.

Knaus, W. 1982. *How to Get Out of a Rut.* Englewood Cliffs, New Jersey: Prentice Hall.

Knaus, W. 2000. *Take Charge Now.* New York: John Wiley and Sons.

Knaus, W., Klarreich, S., Grieger, R., and Knaus, N. 2010. *Fearless Job Hunting.* Oakland: New Harbinger Publications.

Knaus, W. 2012. *The Cognitive Behavioral Workbook for Depression.* 2nd ed. Oakland: New Harbinger Publications.

Korzybski, A. 1933. *Science and Sanity.* New York: The Science Press Printing Company.

Kostewicz, D. E., R. M. Kubina, Jr., and J. O. Cooper. 2000. "Managing Aggressive Thoughts and Feelings with Daily Counts of Non-Aggressive Thoughts and Feelings: A Self-Experiment." *Journal of Behavior Therapy and Experimental Psychiatry* 31 (3–4): 177–187.

Krahé, B., J. Lutz, and I. Sylla. 2018. "Lean Back and Relax: Reclined Seating Position Buffers the Effect of Frustration on Anger and Aggression." *European Journal of Social Psychology.* Abstract.

Krizan, Z., and A. D. Herlache. 2016. "Sleep Disruption and Aggression: Implications for Violence and Its Prevention." *Psychology of Violence* 6: 542–552. http://dx.doi.org/10.1037/vio0000018

Krizan, Z., and G. Hisler. 2019. "Sleepy Anger: Restricted Sleep Amplifies Angry Feelings." *Journal of Experimental Psychology: General* 148 (7): 1239–1250.

Kubzansky L. D., and I. Kawachi. 2000. "Going to the Heart of the Matter: Do Negative Emotions Cause Coronary Heart Disease?" *Journal of Psychosomatic Research* 48 (4–5): 323-337.

Kubzansky, L. D., D. Sparrow, B. Jackson, S. Cohen, S. T. Weiss, and R. J. Wright. 2006. "Angry Breathing: a Prospective Study of Hostility and Lung Function in the Normative Aging Study." *Thorax* 61: 863–68.

Landmann, H., and U. Hess. 2017. "What Elicits Third-Party Anger? The Effects of Moral Violation and Others' Outcome on Anger and Compassion." *Cognition and Emotion* 31 (6): 1097–1111.

Lieberman, M. D., N. I. Eisenberger, M. J. Crockett, S. M. Tom, J. H. Pfeifer, and B. M. Way. 2007. "Putting Feelings into Words: Affect Labeling Disrupts Amygdala Activity in Response to Affective Stimuli." *Psychological Science* 18 (5): 421–428.

Lee, L. O., P. James, E. S. Zevon, E. S. Kim, C. Trudel-Fitzgerald, A. Spiro III, F. Grodstein, and L. D. Kubzansky. 2019. "Optimism Is Associated with Exceptional Longevity in 2 Epidemiologic Cohorts of Men and Women." *PNAS Proceedings of the National Academy of Sciences of the United States of America* 116 (37): 18357–18362.

Lu, X., T. Li, Z. Xia, R. Zhu, L. Wang, Y. J. Luo, and F. Krueger. 2019. "Connectome-Based Model Predicts Individual Differences in Propensity to Trust." *Human Brain Mapping.* Advance online publication.

Lumet, S. *Network.* 1976. Beverly Hills, CA: MGM/United Artists, Film.

Ma-Kellams, C., and J. Lerner. 2016. "Trust Your Gut or Think Carefully? Examining Whether an Intuitive, Versus a Systematic, Mode of Thought Produces Greater Empathic Accuracy." *Journal of Personality and Social Psychology* 111 (5): 674–685.

MacCormack, J. K., and K. A. Lindquist. 2019. "Feeling Hangry? When Hunger Is Conceptualized as Emotion." *Emotion* 19 (2): 301–319.

Mahon, N. E., A. Yarcheski, T. J. Yarcheski, and M. M. Hanks. 2006. "Correlates of Low Frustration Tolerance in Young Adolescents." *Psychological Reports* 99 (1): 230.

Martin, R. C. and E. R. Dahlen. 2004. "Irrational Beliefs and the Experience and Expression of Anger." *Journal of Rational-Emotive and Cognitive-Behavior Therapy* 22(1): 3–20.

McEwen, B., and E. N. Lasley. 2002. *The End of Stress As We Know It.* Washington, DC: The Dana Press.

McEwen, B. S., and N. L. Rasgon. 2018. "The Brain and Body on Stress: Allostatic Load and Mechanisms for Depression and Dementia." In *Depression as a Systemic Illness*, edited by J. J. Strain and M. Blumenfield, 14–36. New York: Oxford University Press.

McGetrick, J., and F. Range. 2018. "Inequity Aversion in Dogs: A Review." *Learning and Behavior* 46: 479–500.

McIntyre, K. M., E. Puterman, J. M. Scodes, T. H. Choo, C. J. Choi, M. Pavlicova, and R. P. Sloan. 2020. "The Effects of Aerobic Training on Subclinical Negative Affect: A Randomized Controlled Trial." *Health Psychology* 39 (4): 255–264.

Melli, G., R. Bailey, C. Carraresi, and A. Poli. 2017. "Metacognitive Beliefs as a Predictor of Health Anxiety in a Self-Reporting Italian Clinical Sample." *Clinical Psychology and Psychotherapy* 25 (2): 263–271.

Muschalla, B., and J. von Kenne. 2020. "What Matters: Money, Values, Perceived Negative Life Events? Explanative Factors in Embitterment." *Psychological Trauma: Theory, Research, Practice, and Policy.* Advance online publication. https://doi.org/10.1037/tra0000547

Okajima, I., and Y. Inoue. 2018. "Efficacy of Cognitive Behavioral Therapy for Comorbid Insomnia: A Meta-Analysis." *Sleep and Biological Rhythms* 16 (1): 21–35.

Okuda, M., J. Picazo, M. Olfson, D. S. Hasin, S. M. Liu, S. Bernardi, and C. Blanco. 2015. "Prevalence and Correlates of Anger in the Community: Results from a National Survey." *CNS Spectrums* 20 (2): 130–139.

Oltean, H. R., P. Hyland, F. Vallières, and D. O. David. 2018. "Rational Beliefs, Happiness and Optimism: An Empirical Assessment of REBT's Model of Psychological Health." *International Journal of Psychology.* Advance online publication.

Payot, J., 1909. *The Education of the Will.* New York: Funk & Wagnalls.

Perciavalle, V., M. Blandini, P. Fecarotta, A. Buscemi, D. Di Corrado, L. Bertolo, F. Fichera, and M. Coco. 2017. "The Role of Deep Breathing on Stress." *Neurological Sciences* 38 (3): 451–458.

Pfattheicher, S., C. Sassenrath, and J. Keller. 2019. "Compassion Magnifies Third-Party Punishment." *Journal of Personality and Social Psychology* 117 (1): 124–141.

Picó-Pérez, M., M. Alemany-Navarro, J. E. Dunsmoor, J. Radua, A. Albajes-Eizagirre, B. Vervliet, N. Cardoner, O. Benet, B. J. Harrison, C. Soriano-Mas, and M. A. Fullana. 2019. "Common and Distinct Neural Correlates of Fear Extinction and Cognitive Reappraisal: A Meta-Analysis of fMRI Studies." *Neuroscience and Biobehavioral Reviews* 104: 102–115.

Popper, K. 1992. *The Logic of Scientific Discovery.* London: Routledge.

Ralston, W. R. S. 1869. *Krilof and His Fables.* London, England: Strahan and Co. Publishers.

Range, F., L. Horn, Z. Viranyi, and L. Huber. 2009. "The Absence of Reward Induces Inequity Aversion in Dogs." *PNAS Proceedings of the National Academy of Sciences of the United States of America* 106 (1): 340–45.

Redding, R E., J. D. Herbert, E. M. Forman, and B. A. Gaudiano. 2008. "Popular Self-Help Books for Anxiety, Depression and Trauma: How Scientifically Grounded and Useful are They?" *Professional Psychology: Research and Practice* 39 (5): 537–545.

Reynolds, E. 1656. *A Treatise of the Passions and Faculties of the Soul of Man, with the Several Dignities and Corruptions Thereunto Belonging.* London, England: Robert Bostock.

Robertson, D. 2010. *The Philosophy of Cognitive-Behavioural Therapy (CBT): Stoic Philosophy as Rational and Cognitive Psychotherapy.* New York: Routledge.

Rosenberg, B. D., and J. T. Siegel. 2018. "A 50-Year Review of Psychological Reactance Theory: Do Not Read This Article." *Motivation Science* 4 (4): 281–300.

Roy, B., A. V. Diez-Roux, T. Seeman, N. Ranjit, S. Shea, and M. Cushman. 2010. "Association of Optimism and Pessimism with Inflammation and Hemostasis in the Multi-Ethnic Study of Atherosclerosis (MESA)." *Psychosomatic Medicine* 72 (2): 134–140.

Salter, A. 1949. *Conditioned Reflex Therapy.* New York: Creative Age Press.

Shuman, E., E. Halperin, and M. Reifen Tagar. 2018. "Anger as a Catalyst for Change? Incremental Beliefs and Anger's Constructive Effects in Conflict." *Group Processes & Intergroup Relations* 21 (7): 1092–1106.

Sloane, S., R. Baillargeon, and D. Premack. 2012. "Do Infants Have a Sense of Fairness?" *Psychological Science* 23 (2): 196–204.

Smaardijk V. R., A. H. Maas, P. Lodder, W. J. Kop, and P. M. Mommersteeg. 2020. "Sex and Gender-stratified Risks of Psychological Factors for Adverse Clinical Outcomes in Patients with Ischemic Heart Disease: A Systematic Review and Meta-Analysis." *International Journal of Cardiology* 302: 21–29.

Sohl, S. J., and A. Moyer. 2009. "Refining the Conceptualization of a Future-Oriented Self-Regulatory Behavior: Proactive Coping." *Personality and Individual Differences* 47 (2): 139–144.

Speed, B. C., B. L. Goldstein, and M. R. Goldfried. 2018. "Assertiveness Training: A Forgotten Evidence-Based Treatment. *Clinical Psychology: Science and Practice* 25 (1): 1–20.

Spinhoven, P., N. Klein, M. Kennis, A. O. J. Cramer, G. Siegle, P. Cuijpers, J. Ormel, S. D. Hollon, and C. L. Bockting. 2018. "The Effects of Cognitive-Behavior Therapy for Depression on Repetitive Negative Thinking: A Meta-Analysis." *Behaviour Research and Therapy* 106: 71–85.

Stavrova, O., and D. Ehlebracht. 2016. "Cynical Beliefs About Human Nature and Income: Longitudinal and Cross-cultural Analyses." *Journal of Personality and Social Psychology* 110 (1): 116–132.

Stevens, S. E., M. T. Hynan, M. Allen, M. M. Braun, and M. R. McCart. 2007. "Are Complex Psychotherapies More Effective Than Biofeedback, Progressive Muscle Relaxation, or Both? A Meta-Analysis." *Psychological Reports* 100 (1): 303–324.

Stravinsky, I. 1947. *Poetics of Music in the Form of Six Lessons.* Translated by A. Knodel and I. Dahl. Cambridge, MA: Harvard University Press.

Suarez, E. C., J. G. Lewis, and C. Kuhn. 2002. "The Relation of Aggression, Hostility, and Anger to Lipopolysaccharide-Stimulated Tumor Necrosis Factor (TNF)-*a* by Blood Monocytes from Normal Men." *Brain, Behavior, and Immunity* 16 (6): 675–684.

Tabibnia, G., and D. Radecki. 2018. "Resilience Training That Can Change the Brain." *Consulting Psychology Journal: Practice and Research* 70 (1): 59–88.

Tafrate, C., and H. Kassinove. 2019. *Anger Management for Everyone*, Oakland, CA: New Harbinger Publications.

Takahashi, A., M. E. Flanigan, B. S. McEwen, and S. J. Russo. 2018. "Aggression, Social Stress, and the Immune System in Humans and Animal Models." *Frontline Behavioral Neuroscience* 12, Article 56. doi: 10.3389/fnbeh.2018.00056. eCollection 2018.

Takebe, M., F. Takahashi, and H. Sato. 2017. The Effects of Anger Rumination and Cognitive Reappraisal on Anger-In and Anger-Control. *Cognitive Therapy and Research* 41 (4): 654–661.

Tang, T. Z., R. J. DeRubeis, R. Beberman, and T. Pham. 2005. "Cognitive Changes, Critical Sessions, and Sudden Gains in Cognitive-Behavioral Therapy for Depression." *Journal of Consulting and Clinical Psychology* 73 (1): 168–172.

Tangney, J. P., D. Hill-Barlow, P. E. Wagner, D. E. Marschall, J. K. Borenstein, J. Sanftner, T. Mohr, and R. Gramzow. 1996. "Assessing Individual Differences in Constructive Versus Destructive Responses to Anger Across the Lifespan." *Journal of Personality and Social Psychology* 70 (4): 780–796.

ten Brinke, L., K. D. Vohs, and D. R. Carney. 2016. "Can Ordinary People Detect Deception After All?" *Trends in Cognitive Sciences* 20 (8): 579–588.

Tracy, F. 1896. *The Psychology of Childhood*. 3rd ed. Boston, MA: D. C. Heath and Co., Publishers.

Troy, A. S., and I. B. Mauss. 2011. "Resilience in the Face of Stress: Emotion Regulation Ability as a Protective Factor." In *Resilience and Mental Health: Challenges Across the Lifespan*. Edited by S. Southwick, B. Litz, D. Charney, and M. Friedman, 30–44. New York: Cambridge University Press.

Troy, A. S., A. J. Shallcross, and I. B. Mauss. 2013. "A Person-by-Situation Approach to Emotion Regulation: Cognitive Reappraisal Can Either Help or Hurt, Depending on the Context." *Psychological Science* 24 (12): 2505–2514.

Twedt, E., R. M. Rainey, and D. R. Proffitt. 2019. "Beyond Nature: The Roles of Visual Appeal and Individual Differences in Perceived Restorative Potential." *Journal of Environmental Psychology* 65, Article 101322.

Vergara, M. D. J. 2020. "The Reduction of Arousal Across Physiological Response Systems: Effects of Single-System Biofeedback, Pattern Biofeedback and Muscle Relaxation." *Dissertation Abstracts International: Section B: The Sciences and Engineering*, 81 (1-B).

Vîslă, A., C. Flückiger, M. grosse Holtforth, and D. David. 2016. "Irrational Beliefs and Psychological Distress: A Meta-Analysis." *Psychotherapy and Psychosomatics* 85 (1): 8–15.

Wang, Y., and A. M. E. Henderson. 2018. "Just Rewards: 17-Month-Old Infants Expect Agents to Take Resources According to the Principles of Distributive Justice." *Journal of Experimental Child Psychology* 172: 25–40.

Wiedemann, M., R. Stott, A. Nickless, E. T. Beierl, J. Wild, E. Warnock-Parkes, N. Grey, D. M. Clark, and A. Ehlers. 2020. "Cognitive Processes Associated with Sudden Gains in Cognitive Therapy for Posttraumatic Stress Disorder in Routine Care." *Journal of Consulting and Clinical Psychology* 88 (5): 455–469.

Williams, J. E., C. C. Paton, I. C. Siegler, M. L. Eigenbrodt, F. J. Nieto, and H. A. Tyroler. 2000. "Anger Proneness Predicts Coronary Heart Disease Risk." *Circulation* 101 (17): 2034–2039.

Williams, T. A. 1914. "A Contrast in Psychoanalysis: Three Cases." *The Journal of Abnormal Psychology* 9 (2–3): 73–86.

Williams, T. 1923. *Dreads and Besetting Fears*. Boston: Little Brown and Company.

Wolpe, J. 1973. *The Practice of Behavior Therapy*. 2nd ed. Elmsford, New York: Pergamon.

Wootton, B. M., S. A. Steinman, A. Czerniawski, K. Norris, C. Baptie, G. Diefenbach, and D. F. Tolin. 2018. "An Evaluation of the Effectiveness of a Transdiagnostic Bibliotherapy Program for Anxiety and Related Disorders: Results from Two Studies Using a Benchmarking Approach." *Cognitive Therapy and Research* 42 (5): 565–580.

Yip, J. A., and M. E. Schweitzer. 2019. "Losing Your Temper and Your Perspective: Anger Reduces Perspective-Taking." *Organizational Behavior and Human Decision Processes* 150: 28–45.

Young, K. S., R. T. LeBeau, A. N. Niles, K. J. Hsu, L. J. Burklund, B. Mesri, D. Saxbe, M. D. Lieberman, and M. G. Craske. 2019. "Neural Connectivity During Affect Labeling Predicts Treatment Response to Psychological Therapies for Social Anxiety Disorder." *Journal of Affective Disorders* 242: 105–110.

Yu, B., M. Funk, J. Hu, and L. Feijs. 2018. "Unwind: A Musical Biofeedback for Relaxation Assistance." *Behaviour & Information Technology* 37 (8): 800–814.

Zaehringer, J., R. Falquez, A. L. Schubert, F. Nees, and S. Barnow. 2018. "Neural Correlates of Reappraisal Considering Working Memory Capacity and Cognitive Flexibility." *Brain Imaging and Behavior*. Advance online publication.

William J. Knaus, EdD, is a licensed psychologist with more than forty-six years of clinical experience working with people suffering from anxiety, depression, and procrastination. He has appeared on numerous regional and national television shows, including *The Today Show*, and more than one hundred radio shows. His ideas have appeared in national magazines such as *U.S. News & World Report* and *Good Housekeeping*, and major newspapers such as *The Washington Post* and the *Chicago Tribune*. He is one of the original directors of postdoctoral psychotherapy training in rational emotive behavior therapy (REBT). Knaus is author or coauthor of more than twenty-five books, including *The Cognitive Behavioral Workbook for Anxiety*, *The Cognitive Behavioral Workbook for Depression*, and *The Procrastination Workbook*.

Foreword writer **Robert Alberti, PhD**, has received international recognition for his writing and editing, which is often praised as the "gold standard" for psychological self-help. Retired from a long career as a psychologist, marriage and family therapist, editor, and publisher, he is author of *Your Perfect Right*, which has sold more than 1.3 million copies in the United States, and has been published in translation in more than twenty languages around the world.

Index

A

ABCDE approach, 45–51; acronym description, 45–47; exercise utilizing, 49–51; process for exploring, 47–49

acceptance: accepting as a solution, 121; characteristics of, 39; My Acceptance exercise, 40–41; as stage of change, 156, 157–158; of troubling thoughts, 113

acceptance and commitment therapy (ACT), 2–3

accommodation stage of change, 156, 157

accusatory language, 143

act perspective, 58–60

action stage of change, 156, 157

activating events, 45–46, 47

active-reflective communications, 141–144; contemplation experiment, 144–145; guidelines for, 142–144; purpose of, 141–142

actualization stage of change, 156, 158

adverse inequity, 71

affect labeling, 16–17, 88

agenda setting, 147–148

aggression: anger and, 11; assertion as substitute for, 130; proactive, 100; shame and, 126

aggressive thoughts, 17–20

Albert Ellis Reader, The (Blau), 171

Alberti, Robert, x, 130

allostatic overload, 97–98

American Psychological Association (APA), 8, 88

amygdala, 16, 73

anger: approaches to combatting, 30–41; assertive solutions for, 129–137, 147; assumptions related to, 139–141; body-mind solutions for, 87–105; communication strategies for, 141–148; cost-benefit analysis of, 167–168, 174; cycle of harmful, 29–30; emergency responses to, 12–25; four views of, 11–12; frustration tolerance and, 107–118; key tenets about, x; mastery over, 151–161; natural vs. parasitic, 7; nine factors characterizing, 10–11; perspective solution for, 55–67; problem-solving solutions for, 119–127; progress log, 26–27; survey on, 8–10; unfairness and, 69–85. See also parasitic anger

anger catastrophizing, 109–113; chart for working with, 111, 112; explanation and example of, 109–110; PURRRRS technique for, 115–117

anger-combatting approaches, 30–41; avoiding fundamental attribution errors, 32–34; breaking free from catharsis, 30–31; escaping the blame trap, 31–32; exploring acceptance views, 39–41; pursuing enlightened self-interest, 41; reappraising situations, 34–38

Anger Management for Everyone (Tafrate & Kassinove), 171

Anxiety Skills Workbook, The (Hofmann), 38

Aristotle, 72

assertive questioning, 145–146

assertiveness, 11, 129–137; anger expression and, 147; complex situations of, 135; creating a philosophy of, 136; experiment for practicing, 132–134; goal technique applied to, 134–135; ten strategies of, 130–131; twelve-step approach to, 131–132

assumptions: examples of making, 139–140; recognizing and checking, 140–141

authenticity, importance of, 143

aversion for unfairness, 70–71

AWARE plan, 173, 174

awareness stage of change, 156

awfulizing, 109

B

beliefs: in ABCDE process, 46, 48; disputing erroneous, 47, 48–49; exploring the power of, 43–45; irrational, 44, 46, 51; uncovering anger-related, 45

bibliotherapy, 3

blame: escaping the trap of, 31–32; externalizing, 46; and no-blame way, 5; parasitic, 10

blame-labeling, 58, 143

Blau, Shawn, 171

Block, Joel, 94

body language, 143

body scanning, 103

body, mind, patterns, and connections approach, 114–115

Bourland, D. David, 57

breathing deeply, 93–94

Buddhist teachings, 2

C

calamity-howling, 109

calming the body, 90–94; deep breathing for, 93–94; progressive muscle relaxation for, 91–93; serenity scenes for, 90–91

Casriel, Dan, 30

catastrophizing, 109

catharsis, breaking free from, 30–31

CBT. See cognitive behavioral therapy

change: five stages of, 156–159; program for moving forward with, 158–159; restrictions related to, 159–160

character overgeneralizations, 57

cheating, example of, 71

choice, recognizing, 173–174

circular reasoning, 56–57

clarity: rephrasing statements for, 142–143; three questions for, 75–76

cognitive behavioral therapy (CBT): bibliotherapy based on, 3; brief history of, 1–3; learning and practicing methods of, 4; research support for, 3

cognitive reappraisal, 34, 36–38, 88

cognitive signatures, 32, 108

Cohen, Elliot D., 168

combatting anger. See anger-combatting approaches

communication strategies, 141–148; active-reflective communications, 141–144; assertive questioning, 145–146; contemplation experiment, 144–145; escalation ladder plan, 147; setting the agenda, 147–148

confident composure, 66

consequences, 46–47, 48

contemplation experiment, 144–145

contingent worth, 126

contrast chart, 79

coping, proactive, 66

coping statements, 153–156, 165

core issues and solutions, 24–25

coronary heart disease (CHD), 97–100; allostatic overload factor in, 97–98; anger factors related to, 98–100. See also heart health

cost-benefit analysis of anger, 167–168, 174

Cotterell, Norman, 173

counting thoughts, 17–21

coverups, 71

cuteness technique, 103

cynical distrust, 99

D

Damasio, Antonio, 152

dangerous mind places, 125

deception, 71, 72

deep breathing, 93–94

demandingness: parasitic anger and, 75; preference thinking vs., 78, 79; questions for clarity about, 75–76

direction of anger, 12

disputing erroneous beliefs, 47, 48–49

distancing yourself from anger, 38

distributive fairness, 72

distrust: cynical, 99; factors related to, 74

double troubles, 113–114

dual process theory, 152

Dubois, Paul, 43

Dunlap, Knight, 13

E

Edison, Thomas, 5
effects, creating new, 47, 49
Ellis, Albert, ix, 4, 39, 45, 51, 75, 109, 171, 174
emergency responses to anger, 12–27; core solutions, 24–25; empirical solutions, 21–23; practical solutions, 14–21; walking solution, 12–14
Emmons, Michael, 130
emotions: expressing, 31; naming, 16–17, 124
empathy, 32, 171–172
empirical solutions, 21–23
enlightened self-interest, 41
Epictetus, ix
E-prime thinking, 57, 58
equality fairness, 72
escalation ladder plan, 147
excesses, blame, 31
exercise: discharging anger through, 31, 170; positive effects of, 114
exonerations, blame, 31, 32
expectations vs. reality, 168–169
exploitation, 71, 72
explosive anger, 124–125
expressed hostility, 99
extensions of blame, 31–32, 33, 57

F

fact-based beliefs, 44
failure, and no-failure way, 5
fairness: irrational demands for, 75; systems of, 72–73; trust related to, 73. See also unfairness
false assumptions, 140
favoritism, example of, 71
15-Minute Relationship Fix, The (Block), 94
flight of angry thoughts technique, 103
Frankl, Viktor, 130
Franklin, Ben, 143
freedom by restriction, 159–160
Freud, Sigmund, 151

frustration: anger and low tolerance for, 108–114; building high tolerance for, 114–118; preparing for provocations and, 165–166
fundamental attribution errors, 32–34

G

Garcia, Ed, 12
Garcy, Pamela D., 170
general semantics, 57
goal technique, 134–135
Golden, William L., 165
Grieger, Russell, 167
guided reappraisals, 34

H

habit, anger as, 12
Hayes, Steven, 2
heart health, 97–104; allostatic overload and, 97–98; anger factors affecting, 98–100; healthy heart program for, 100–102; mindfulness methods for, 102, 103; optimism related to, 104
hidden agendas, 147
Hofmann, Stefan, 3, 38
homework assignments, 4
Horney, Karen, 75
horse-and-rider metaphor, 151
hostility, 11, 99
humorous exaggerations, 65
hypotheses, 134

I

imagery techniques, 103, 165, 171
impulse vs. reason, 151
inequity, aversion to, 70–71
inquiry questions, 60, 61
Inquisitive Man, The (Krilof), 72
insomnia, 94–95
invisible elephant concept, 72
irrational beliefs, 44, 46, 51
is of identity perspective, 57–59

J

Jackobson, Edmund, 91
Janov, Arthur, 30
Johnston, Paul, 57
Jones, Deacon, 31–32

K

Kahneman, Daniel, 152
Kassinove, Howard, 171
Kelly, George, 123
Kirk, Tammy Jo, 57
Klarreich, Sam, 163
Knaus, William, 103
Korzybski, Alfred, 57
Krilof, Ivan, 72

L

labeling emotions, 16–17, 124
language: accusatory, 143; deceptive, 72; preference, 76–77
Lazarus, Arnold, 2
logotherapy, 130
long-term perspective, 63, 64
low frustration tolerance (LFT), 108–114; anger catastrophizing and, 109–113; double troubles and, 113–114; explanation of, 108

M

Making Peace with Imperfection (Cohen), 168
mantra meditation, 103
McEwen, Bruce, 102
meaningfulness, 174–175
memory, impeded by anger, 11
mental karate, 5
metacognitive beliefs, 44
mindfulness methods, 102, 103
mindfulness-based cognitive behavior therapy (MBCBT), 3
mirror exercise, 169
multi-modal therapy (MMT), 2
My Acceptance exercise, 40–41

N

naming emotions, 16–17, 124
natural anger, 7, 10
nature scenes, 90–91
negative affect, 99
negative thoughts, 44, 114, 169
Network (film), 30
no-blame way, 5
no-failure way, 5
nonaggressive thoughts, 17–20

O

objective self-observation, 66
optimism, realistic, 66, 104
overgeneralizing, 57–60; description of, 57–58; experiment on, 58–59

P

parasitic anger, 1; cycle of, 29–30; demandingness and, 75; harmfulness of, 10; key questions about, 13–14; natural anger vs., 7
parasitic blame, 10
parasitic rules, 51–52
parasympathetic nervous system, 91
Patrick, Danica, 57
perfectionistic expectations, 168–169
personal construct therapy, 123
personal situation view, 33
perspective: constrictions on, 56–60; empathy related to, 172; is of identity vs. act, 58–60; narrowed by anger, 55; short- vs. long-term, 63–64
pessimism, 99, 104
pink elephant problem, 96
Popper, Karl, 72
positive perspective triad, 66
practical experiments, 14–21; naming your emotion, 16–17; sitting at the right angle, 14–15; thought-counting technique, 17–21
practical fairness, 73
Practitioner's Guide to Anger Management, The (Kassinove & Tafrate), 171

preference thinking: demandingness vs., 78, 79; reducing anger through, 76–77

prefrontal cortex, 16

preparation way, 5

Pressure Proofing (Klarreich), 163

primal scream therapy, 30–31

priming coping statements, 153–154

proactive aggression, 100

proactive coping, 66

probability option, 51–52

problem finding, 119–120

problem solutions: for explosive anger, 124–125; for shame anger, 125–126

problem solving: experiment for working on, 122–123; rescripting exercise related to, 123–124; in RICP method, 165; steps in process of, 120–121

procedural fairness, 72

Prochaska, Jane, 31–32

progress log, 26–27

progressive muscle relaxation, 91–93

protection, anger as, 12

provocations, preparing for, 165–166

PURRRRS technique, 115–117

Q

questioning techniques, 60–62; assertive questioning, 145–146; experiment exploring, 61–62; inquiry questions, 60, 61; strategy questions, 60–61

questions: on agendas, 147; on assertiveness, 131; on assumptions, 141; on demandingness, 75–76; disputing irrational beliefs, 47, 50; harnessing the power of, 163–164; on parasitic anger, 13–14; PURRRRS technique, 116, 117; reappraisal, 34–36; stages of change, 158–159; on unfairness, 82

R

rational emotive behavior therapy (REBT), 45, 174

rational emotive imagery (REI), 171

reactance anger, 83–84

Reagan, Ronald, 75

realistic expectations, 168–169

realistic optimism, 66, 104

reappraisal strategy, 34–38; cognitive reappraisal experiment, 36–37; guided reappraisals, 34–36

reason vs. impulse, 151

reasoning, circular, 56–57

REBT Super-Activity Guide, The (Garcy), 170

rectifying wrongs, 80, 81

Redding, Richard, 3

reflex theory of anger, 46

relaxation: deep breathing for, 93–94; progressive muscle, 91–93; in RICP method, 165

remedying unfairness, 81

rescripting exercise, 123–124

resolving problems, 81

response cost, 81

restriction, freedom by, 159–160

retaliation, 81, 99

retribution, 81, 82

revenge, 81, 82

Reynolds, Edward, 70

Richardson, Roberta Galluccio, 169

Richman, Diana R., 172

RICP method, 165–166

role reversal question, 49

Rudolph, Jeff, 147

rules: fairness, 73; parasitic, 51–52

rumination, 98

Russell, Bertrand, 44

S

Scream Away from Happiness, A (Casriel), 30

scripts, changing, 123–124

Segal, Zindel, 3

self-defeating patterns, 114

self-importance, 113

self-interest fairness, 73

self-mastery, 4

self-observation, 66

serenity scenes, 90–91

Serious Business of Being Happy, The (Grieger), 167

7-R Action Plan, 80–83

shame, anger and, 125–126

short-term perspective, 63, 64

signal, anger as, 11

Singer, William "Rick," 71

sitting at the right angle, 14–15

situational reappraisal, 34–38

sleep, 94–97; body-calming methods for, 97; insomnia and problems with, 94–95; pink elephant problem and, 96; strategies promoting, 95–96

smiling in the mirror technique, 169

social fairness systems, 72–73

Socrates and Socratic questioning, 1–2

stages of change, 156–159

Stoics, 1, 2

strategy questions, 60–61

stress: APA survey on, 8, 88; cycle of anger and, 87–88; glass metaphor for, 89–90; rating level of, 88–89

supportive people, 114–115

suppressed hostility/anger, 99

survey on anger, 8–10

symptom, anger as, 11

System 1 and System 2 thinking, 152–153

T

Teasdale, John, 3

tension tolerance, 107, 108

tension-anger spinoff effect, 108

terrible triangle, 80

terrific triangle, 80

third-party reactance, 84

thought-counting technique, 17–21

thoughts: acceptance of troubling, 113; aggressive vs. nonaggressive, 17–20; deescalating, 114; negative, 44, 114, 169; parasitic rules and, 51; preference, 76–77, 78

3-D rational emotive imagery, 171

top tips: on anger-fear puzzle, 12; on breathing deeply, 94; on cost-benefit analysis of anger, 167–168; on dangerous mind places, 125; on disengaging your angry brain, 170–171; on distancing yourself from anger, 38; on empathy and perspective, 171–172; on expectations vs. reality, 168–169; on expressing anger assertively, 147; on harnessing the power of questions, 163–164; on practicing mindfulness techniques, 103; on preparing for provocations and frustrations, 165–166; on recognizing your choice, 173–174; on smiling in the mirror, 169; on stopping and thinking it out, 172–173; on 3-D rational emotive imagery, 171; on uncovering anger beliefs, 45

Tracy, Frederick, 7

trust: fairness related to, 73; seven factors of, 73–74; verifying, 74–75

tunnel vision, 11, 55

tyranny of the should, 75

U

unconditional acceptance, 39

unfairness: anger toward, 69, 75, 80, 83–84; aversion for, 70–71; definition of, 70; distrust related to, 74; effort needed to rectify, 80; processes of, 71; reactance to, 83–84; response options, 81–83. See also fairness

V

venting, 31

W

walking solution, 12–14

website for book, 1

Williams, Tom, 109

Wolpe, Joseph, 91, 165

Y

Y choice, 152–153

Your Perfect Right (Alberti & Emmons), 130, 148

MORE BOOKS from
NEW HARBINGER PUBLICATIONS

THE HIGH-CONFLICT COUPLE

A Dialectical Behavior Therapy Guide to Finding Peace, Intimacy & Validation

978-1572244504 / US $17.95

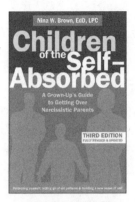

CHILDREN OF THE SELF-ABSORBED, THIRD EDITION

A Grown-Up's Guide to Getting Over Narcissistic Parents

978-1572245617 / US $17.95

THE JEALOUSY CURE

Learn to Trust, Overcome Possessiveness & Save Your Relationship

978-1626259751 / US $16.95

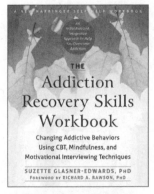

THE ADDICTION RECOVERY SKILLS WORKBOOK

Changing Addictive Behaviors Using CBT, Mindfulness & Motivational Interviewing Techniques

978-1626252783 / US $25.95

THE UPWARD SPIRAL

Using Neuroscience to Reverse the Course of Depression, One Small Change at a Time

978-1626251205 / US $17.95

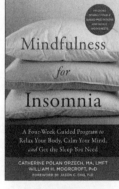

MINDFULNESS FOR INSOMNIA

A Four-Week Guided Program to Relax Your Body, Calm Your Mind & Get the Sleep You Need

978-1684032587 / US $16.95

newharbingerpublications

1-800-748-6273 / newharbinger.com

(VISA, MC, AMEX / prices subject to change without notice)

Follow Us 🅾 ⬜ 🐦 ▶ 📌 in

Don't miss out on new books in the subjects that interest you.
Sign up for our **Book Alerts** at **newharbinger.com/bookalerts**

Register your **new harbinger** titles for additional benefits!

When you register your **new harbinger** title—purchased in any format, from any source—you get access to benefits like the following:

- Downloadable accessories like printable worksheets and extra content

- Instructional videos and audio files

- Information about updates, corrections, and new editions

Not every title has accessories, but we're adding new material all the time.

Access free accessories in 3 easy steps:

1. Sign in at NewHarbinger.com (or **register** to create an account).

2. Click on **register a book**. Search for your title and click the **register** button when it appears.

3. Click on the **book cover or title** to go to its details page. Click on **accessories** to view and access files.

That's all there is to it!

If you need help, visit:

NewHarbinger.com/accessories

new harbinger
CELEBRATING
40 YEARS